he Changing Face of Church

he Changing Face of Church

EMERGING MODELS OF PARISH LEADERSHIP

Marti R. Jewell and David A. Ramey

EMERGING MODELS
OF PASTORAL LEADERSHIP

A Joint Project, Funded by the Lilly Endowment, Inc.

LOYOLAPRESS.
A JESUIT MINISTRY
Chicago

Partnering for Pastoral Excellence

National Association for Lay Ministry | Conference for Pastoral Planning and Council Development | National Association of Church Personnel Administrators | National Association of Diaconate Directors | National Catholic Young Adult Ministry Association NCYAMA | National Federation of Priests Councils

LOYOLAPRESS.
A JESUIT MINISTRY

3441 N. Ashland Avenue
Chicago, Illinois 60657
(800) 621-1008
www.loyolapress.com

Cover image Lars Hammar
Cover design by Kathryn Seckman Kirsch and Mia McGloin
Interior design by Maggie Hong

Library of Congress Cataloging-in-Publication Data
Jewell, Marti R.
  The changing face of church : emerging models of parish leadership / Marti R. Jewell and David A. Ramey.
    p. cm.
  ISBN-13: 978-0-8294-2647-2
  ISBN-10: 0-8294-2647-7
  1. Parishes—United States. 2. Christian leadership—United States.
  3. Pastoral theology—United States. 4. Catholic Church—United States.
  5. Christian leadership—Catholic Church. 6. Pastoral theology—Catholic
  Church. I. Ramey, David A., 1951- II. Title.
  BX1407.P3J48 2010
  254'.020973—dc22
                                                                      2009038853

Printed in the United States of America
10 11 12 13 14 15 Versa 10 9 8 7 6 5 4 3 2 1

Contents

Introduction

A paradigm shift is taking place in Catholic parishes. Structures are changing, leadership roles are evolving, and pastoral practices are being adapted. Faced with unanticipated challenges in the midst of changing demographics and world-views, parishes are becoming "total ministering communities" in which the faithful, lay and ordained, share in the sacramental, pastoral, and catechetical care of the community. Parishioners are offering their talents to the service of the church. Pastors are taking on more and more parishes, and parish staffs are growing. New ministries are flourishing. At the same time, the church is experiencing demographic changes that mirror the current immigration trends in the United States, especially as they relate to Spanish-speaking communities. While there are those who long for the certainty of earlier eras, the changes continue, generating new opportunities for growth and creativity, as well as new organizational forms. The emergent pastoral leaders are redefining themselves within a new mind-set, finding creative and adaptive responses to the needs of the parish community.

In order to identify and share these emerging patterns, the Emerging Models of Pastoral Leadership Project hosted more than five hundred people in a series of eight regional leadership gatherings throughout the United States between November 2004 and November 2006.[1] The intention of the symposia process was to identify typical pastoral leadership structures and experiences that might provide a benchmark for leadership in parishes throughout the United States.

Participants, identified by their dioceses as the thought-leaders in the field, were invited to share their experience and knowledge. In all, 82 percent completed extensive questionnaires involving over twenty-seven items describing their current experiences and expectations for the future. Participants included pastors, parish life coordinators, deacons, pastoral associates, parish pastoral council reps, and diocesan leaders in their various roles and responsibilities. The representation of men and women in these symposia was nearly equal. The age distribution of symposia participants reflected the current profiles of church leaders with 67 percent of participants being between the ages of fifty and sixty-nine. Disappointingly, there was an underrepresentation of multicultural pastoral leaders, as well as young adults.

Symposia participants also represented a balanced distribution of parish households, with approximately 46 percent serving over 1,200 households and an equal percentage serving under 1,200. Over 70 percent of symposia participants had achieved a master's or doctoral degree during their careers. About half of symposia participants represented parishes with pastors responsible for one parish, while a large number represented more diverse leadership models.

Findings

Throughout the symposia process, it became apparent that the results of the initiative would be substantially different from anticipated. While we had expected to identify a handful of emerging structural models and defined roles of parish leaders (e.g., megachurches, multiple parish pastors), the project found little consistency and uniformity among these emerging models. The surprising diversity is largely driven by the economics, geography, and demographics of the local situation. Preferred ecclesiologies or diocesan planning efforts did not appear as a significant factor in determining how parish structures and leadership are evolving among symposia cohorts. A total of seven structural models of parish leadership were identified throughout the symposia process, with seemingly infinite variations. Across these parish structures pastoral leaders are developing new models of pastoral leadership through

- intentional planning and visioning processes in parishes;
- innovative approaches to clustering parishes and interparish collaboration;
- intentional formation of lay leaders;
- concentration on smaller, more intentional faith communities within the parish, providing outreach to individuals and families.

Amazingly, the practices and experiences of these lay and ordained pastoral leaders are similar in many ways despite their geographic, economic, cultural, and demographic diversity. These similarities have caused the project to redefine emerging models as less of a "structural model" and more of "a set of practices" which are giving birth to the parish of the future. The twelve most evident common elements include the following:

- sacramentality of parish life as a eucharistic community
- total ministering communities
- formation of lay ministers

- pastor or parish life coordinator as agent of change
- pastoral staff as leadership team that calls forth the ministry of the community
- emergent multiculturalism as grace
- lifelong catechesis
- intentional and proactive outreach to individuals and households
- regional ministry to youth and young adults
- regional collaboration among parishes
- structural commitment to justice
- accountability and transparency in parish administration

Results

The responses of these thought leaders revealed a portrait of the changing landscape of parish life, spotlighting evolving and adaptive models of parish leadership, as well as creative organizational structures. They pointed toward a transformation in parish life marked by deep change. Despite the complexity of the challenges they face, the symposia participants demonstrated a strong sense of optimism in the spiritual vitality of their parishes. To proclaim the gospel in a changing world and provide for the pastoral care of the people of God, the Catholic Church is heeding the call of Pope John Paul II in *Novo Millennio Ineunte*:

> [Need] must be translated into pastoral initiatives adapted to the circumstances of each community . . . It is in the local churches that the specific features of a detailed pastoral plan can be identified—goals and methods,

formation and enrichment of the people involved, the search for the necessary resources—which will enable the proclamation of Christ to reach people, mould communities, and have a deep and incisive influence in bringing Gospel values to bear in society and culture.

I therefore earnestly exhort the Pastors of the particular Churches, with the help of all sectors of God's People, confidently to plan the stages of the journey ahead, harmonizing the choices of each diocesan community with those of neighboring Churches and of the universal Church . . . What awaits us therefore is an exciting work of pastoral revitalization—a work involving all of us.[2]

As pastors, parish staff, and parishioners seek to understand the need in today's world, reflect on that need in the light of the Gospel and our tradition, and respond to that need in ways that serve God's people, they are developing truly creative practices. This book is designed to share with you the insights, practices, and theology of the symposia participants, which, in themselves, should offer no surprises. You will find much of your work affirmed in these pages, since time-honored practices continue in use and are being adapted to fit the changing needs of certain parishes or regions. What we hope to share with you is the optimism and creativity that these participants have brought to the enterprise, inviting you to explore your own ideas and innovations.

We believe that this sharing of the experience of pastoral leaders throughout the country represents a significant contribution to the emerging understanding of the direction of parish life. Throughout the book, we have presented the thoughts, hopes, and dreams of pastoral leaders in their own words. We have found their realism and sober optimism inspirational, even prophetic, and their story has seemed to us an interesting counterpoint to the perception of a church in decline. A parish life coordinator from the Mid-Atlantic region of the United States captured the findings and essence of her colleagues and the project in the following words:

> The parish will be a community of communities which gather together on Sunday mornings to celebrate Eucharist and go forth from the tables to build the reign of God's justice and peace in the larger community of the city, state, country, and the world. The parish will understand that it does not exist for itself, but for the mission. Parish = communion and mission.

I

SPIRITUALLY ALIVE AND HEALTHY PARISHES

The Context for Parish Ministry

What do pastoral leaders in the United States see for the parish of the future? Through a series of eight regional symposia conducted between November 2004 and November 2006, the Emerging Models of Pastoral Leadership Project asked five hundred pastoral leaders for their views. These symposia gathered leading-edge, grassroots pastoral leaders who were identified by their dioceses to participate in a three-day gathering. Structured questions were used at these symposia to evaluate and detect emerging trends in pastoral life and emerging leadership for the Catholic community in the United States.

The pastoral leaders identified many pressures that have an impact on parishes. For instance, parishes are faced with increasing financial pressures to maintain their viability as are other not-for-profit organizations. In addition, parishes in metropolitan areas often face changing demographics as the Catholic population disperses and, in many cases, shifts to the suburbs and to the South and to the West. Many dioceses have an abundance of physical assets in locations that are poor, underserved, and no longer Catholic. These dioceses also lack adequate capital to build new churches and schools where Catholics have moved.

Parish schools are struggling with their vitality and identity, with 845 schools or 11.5 percent closing over the past ten years.[3] New models and structures for parish schools are being considered throughout the United States. The availability of priests to serve local parishes is a powerful driver for the future context, structure, and vitality of parish ministries. Parishes are also facing a nationwide decline in Mass attendance and the residual effects of national publicity about the sexual abuse of minor children by priests.

In light of these conditions, one might expect that pastoral leaders would take a decidedly unfavorable view of their parish and its future viability. However, a steady, sober, and optimistic vision of the vitality and context of parish life emerged among symposia participants.

When discussing the current context of parish ministry and its vitality, symposia participants were asked to look at three factors. First, they considered a spiritually alive and healthy community represented by vibrant participation and celebration of the Eucharist and sacraments. Second, participants were asked to consider the visible commitments within their parishes to building the life of the faith community, with a demonstrated involvement of parishioners in ministries of the word, worship, and service within the church and beyond to the larger community. Finally, participants were asked to consider the concept of a total ministering community, which involves the leadership of pastors, pastoral staff, and pastoral council members working together to forge a vision of the parish.

Figure 1 (see page 16) indicates the importance symposia participants place on these three leadership elements of parish life. It is clear that parish ministers recognize the importance of these attributes as contributing to the vitality and future stability of parish life.

Figure 2 (see page 17) represents their assessment of the current effectiveness of their parishes in demonstrating these elements of pastoral leadership. The majority of participants represent their parishes as effective or very effective in this regard. Their assessment of effectiveness trails behind their assessment of the importance of these factors.

Figure 3 (see page 17) shows participants' level of confidence in their parish becoming a vibrant faith community in the future. Clearly, the overwhelming majority of pastoral leaders were confident or very confident concerning their potential to maintain a sense of vitality despite the economic, demographic, structural, and ecclesial conditions they face.

While pastoral leaders in the symposia may not represent an accurate national sampling of all parishes, a decidedly stable yet optimistic view of the context of parish life is represented by their self-assessment of their parishes and their work across parishes in their various dioceses.

What do these pastoral leaders see that enables them to maintain a sense of optimism and sober direction for the future of their parishes while external conditions, such as parish finances, parish structures, and the availability of clergy, seem to indicate a potential decline in parish life? Throughout symposia comments and written responses, three characteristics of the changing context of parish life emerged as the basis of their optimism. These attributes of parish life may provide a helpful understanding of the current and future context of the parish. A former secretary of health, education, and welfare, John Gardner once observed, "Anyone whoever achieved anything of significance had far more hope than the facts justified."[4]

Following are the characteristics that serve as the foundation for optimism and receive the greatest attention, in order of their significance for the future:

- increased involvement of the laity as disciples
- increased cultural diversity contributing to parish vitality
- intentional parish planning and visioning

Increased Involvement of the Laity as Disciples

Pastoral leaders appear to have a keen awareness of the culture-changing impact of the increased involvement and leadership of laity in parish life. In the eyes of these leaders, lay engagement and involvement in parish life was not simply a matter of expediency, but a question of call, vision, and the realization of a mature church in the twenty-first century. As one pastoral leader observed:

> More and more it is clear to me that lay leadership is a necessity, not a nicety! How we can overcome the "fear factor" is a big question, for we need to convince pastors that they are not being threatened—they are being assisted! We stress that the emerging role of the laity is part of their baptismal call! This is so dependent, however, upon relationship! (Pastoral Leader, Southeast)

Throughout its history, the church has endorsed the notion of laity as disciples to the world. In this image of discipleship, the laity is called to fulfill that baptismal mission to renew the world and make disciples of all nations. This sense of lay ministry continues to be a critical dynamic for lay involvement in parish life. These pastoral leaders see the laity's involvement as an equally vital component that informs the life of the faith community. To them, this emphasis on a "lay ministry" for the life of the church is not simply a matter of filling in for unavailable clergy but of the church's full realization of its call to renew not only the world but also itself. The following comments are representative of how pastoral leaders feel about the emergence of new forms of lay leadership in pastoral life:

> We are only seventeen months into our new leadership of PLC/sacramental minister/canonical pastor. One of the two areas in the diocese to have a PLC, we are the first to have a laywoman. Our parishes see themselves as laying groundwork for the future. I think that calls us to regularly evaluate what we are doing, why, and how. We all want to do it well—not only for ourselves, but for other parishes in the diocese who will undergo change in the near future. (Parish Life Coordinator, North Central)

> People are identifying new areas of ministry which need to be developed and are offering expertise for their accomplishment. As we decrease the number of priests and sisters on staff, we are seeing the laity competently step up to the plate. (Pastor, Mid-Atlantic)

> I hope in time that a more collaborative model will emerge where the leadership comes from the people with the pastor's oversight. I hope that the staff will be seen more as a resource to this leadership rather than a substitute for it. I hope that this style of leadership will

foster a growing sense of communion among all of us which is then the reference for all that we do and how we decide new directions. (Pastor, Mid-Atlantic)

At a time when some dioceses are required to diminish their financial investment in lay formation programs, the need is growing even stronger in all sectors of parish life for emerging models of lay pastoral leadership. This need is particularly acute when ministering to multicultural groups and young adults.

The emergence of a Latino community is helping change to a shared ministry style of leadership. Their presence is not a threat to most Anglos there and their "family type" involvement is having an impact on the whole parish. (Pastor, Mid-Atlantic)

There are a larger number of young people of both genders who do not desire to be priests but who are confused by the choices between very authoritarian models and communal models of church leadership. Though they may tend to the more traditional "Father decides" approach to parish life, they primarily want the church to settle on one model and they don't much care which as long as it's stable. There are many who get to know the communal model of parish leadership that our parish follows and come to like it. They are very frustrated, even to the point of ceasing to be active parish members, when they cannot find the model they have experienced here after graduating and moving on. These young adults know what they want but they are unsure of how to bring it about if there is no parish leadership that shares their views. I would like to say that our parish's model will emerge as the standard, and in the long run, I believe it will. In the short run, however, I am not sure. (Pastoral Associate, Upper Midwest)

These pastoral leaders are highly encouraged when they see formal leaders, such as priests, vicars, and bishops, encouraging and supporting these efforts. This not only validates their experience of the vitality of lay leadership in parish life, but also provides them with a needed sense of confidence that their efforts are on the right track and consistent with the goals of the local church.

More collaboration among deaneries/vicariates is needed. There is a need to assist leadership that is stuck in old models, fearful of what is happening and [without] the resources to respond, losing parishioners because of poor leadership. Use present structures like deaneries/vicariates to cross-fertilize the good things that are happening through good leadership with those places where leadership is poor, paralyzed, or stuck. The cross-fertilization that is happening here is a good model. (Diocesan Representative, Northeast)

Our new bishop is trying hard to affect the mindset and systems necessary for good shared leadership on every level of diocesan and parish life. He misses no opportunity to talk about the role of all the baptized and the necessity of living with the heart and mind of Jesus. He is insisting on faith formation and spiritual formation of adults (in the spirit of Vatican II). Ultimately, this will open us to new models. (Diocesan Representative, Mid-Atlantic)

This visible, tangible, and consistent emphasis on the engagement of lay leaders as disciples is a palpable characteristic of parishes represented in the symposia that have a sense of vitality and optimism for the future.

Hopefully, we will continue to see the ascendancy of the laity and the renewed confidence in the indispensable ministry of lay and clergy ministers. I would hope we would be communities driven by a clear mission to continue the work of Jesus Christ to sanctify, teach, and lead persons to faith and eternal life. Concretely, this occurs, hopefully, through vibrant liturgy, education, and mission. (Pastor, North Central)

I think we can expect a greater participation in leadership from the laity and should be preparing them and the community at large for the possibilities. Our church will survive and it will change. The greatest thing we can do is keep reminding people that change is inevitable and pray as a community that the spirit will guide the parish and inspire and call leaders. We also need to help people remember we are part of a worldwide community. As change occurs, it would be beneficial if collaboration extended beyond parish boundaries within the U.S. and drew upon the wisdom of the church leadership in other countries. (Pastoral Council Member, Northeast)

Increased Cultural Diversity Contributing to Parish Vitality

Participants saw the increased presence of diverse cultures in parish life not simply as a challenge to service through day-to-day ministries, but as a transformational element contributing to parish vitality. Symposia participants often reflected how the hopefulness and substantive contributions of diverse cultures have improved their parish life. Undoubtedly, parishes are challenged with bilingual and multilingual forms of worship, different cultural norms for how communities organize, and different socioeconomic implications which result from their multicultural populations. One parish life coordinator reflected upon a poor urban church in a large megalopolis with over twenty native languages represented among parishioners. Yet consistently throughout the symposia, pastoral leaders spoke of a driving vitality that multiculturalism brings to parish identity.

> The Spanish-speaking community is giving me the most hope. We are forming leaders in Ignatian prayer/discernment; we are educating them very basically in theology, pastoral skills, Scripture, liturgy; we are working on building a Catholic school to include children of Hispanic families by day, and their parents by night (ESL, citizenship, literacy)—involving both English and Spanish-speaking communities. (Parish Life Coordinator, Pacific Northwest)

The multicultural and ethnic impact on parish life is far more of a blessing and an opportunity than a problem to be solved or an issue to be addressed. Those pastoral leaders from the symposia who have been able to experience multicultural-ism in parish life as a transformational element see this as an essential contribution to the future of parish vitality. One large suburban parish in the Southeast has introduced bilin-gual worship practices, not because of the current population of Hispanics, but in anticipation and welcome of that future presence. Pastoral leaders frequently described multicultural-ism as an expression of parish vitality.

> I see a place where people of diverse cultures can come together as one faith community; where people are truly invested in the welfare of the church; where fewer clergy and religious focus more on building up the leaders than actually doing particular ministries; where the Eucharist and a mission-based spirituality are the focus of a community's life and well-being. (Pastor, Mid-Atlantic)

> Probably something we can't imagine. I hope it will be a welcoming, inclusive, multicultural community with small faith-sharing groups of all kinds who evangelize their constituencies at work as in their neighborhoods. Prayerful, inclusive liturgy (hopefully eucharistic) with good music and preaching where we recognize and celebrate important moments in people's lives and care for one another; a community that can sustain itself, serve the poor and weak for justice and systemic change, of whom is said, "See how they love one another." (Parish Life Coordinator, Pacific Northwest)

Intentional Parish Planning and Visioning

Those pastoral leaders throughout the symposia who demonstrated a more confident view of the vitality of parish life also stressed the importance of their current and future pastoral planning and visioning processes. In the field of organizational behavior and development, a commitment to planning is often linked to success in high-performing organizations. This disciplined approach to anticipating the future—realigning current structures and service delivery models and crafting a plan of action—is an attribute of effective leadership. Pastoral leaders in the symposia illustrated this practice which is well documented in other social sectors and organizational disciplines.

Pastoral leaders described different, but not dissimilar, approaches to pastoral planning and visioning. Their organizational processes almost always place the pastoral council in a visioning and planning role and often result in increased lay involvement on various task forces and boards which contribute to, and demonstrate, leadership. These processes also often include the formation of new structures and new approaches to teaming and providing needed support both within and beyond the parish.

One very large parish of over 6,000 households in the Northeast has structured its pastoral planning process through lay parish boards with direct responsibility for various aspects of parish life. In this model, the lay parish board develops a plan for the future, assigns budgeted resources, and oversees the implementation of various projects and programs. This lay-led approach to pastoral planning is an example of the extent to which healthy parishes have found a way to integrate organizational "best practices" into their parish formational efforts. However diverse their approach, pastoral leaders frequently expressed a commitment to parish visioning as vital to their future parish communities.

I pray we can select (discern) more visioning and planning parishioners for our pastoral council. The council and staff can then develop and articulate the parish mission. They can tap the parishioners with the right talents to develop ministries. Perhaps a staff member can serve as ministries coordinator so more parishioners can give their gifts, time, and resources to the community. (Diocesan Representative, Southwest)

The two parishes, because of the experience of shared staff and the fact that all ministries I have initiated have been joint, are learning to look beyond "parish as universe unto itself," to a broader vision of church and of parishes cooperating in collaborative ministries and outreach. This is also being promoted through their participation in a multi-parish joint planning process spearheaded by our pastor. (Pastoral Associate, Upper Midwest)

I'm just forging ahead with a "ministry team" model, inviting parishioners to form ministry teams; training and forming them; grounding their understanding of their ministry in Catholic teaching; developing goals and objectives; planning, implementing, and evaluating programs and efforts. So far, I have started a Baptism Ministry Team, Youth Ministry Team, Welcoming Ministry Team, and

Adult Education Ministry Team. The teams are beginning to collaborate with one another to plan and implement events. I am learning more myself (attended Called & Gifted Workshop) about how to help people discern their baptismal call and gifts, so ministries can be formed around the gifts present in the community. (Pastoral Associate, Upper Midwest)

The parish is currently working on our next five-year plan. We are surveying, interviewing, and holding a town hall meeting. When all this is gathered, the pastoral council, staff, and other leadership will set goals in all areas of parish life. We are being connected with our faith tradition as we transition into the next five years. The process has been very energizing for the lay leaders and me. Moving intentionally from "information gathering" to "implementation" will be a key to success. (Pastoral Associate, Upper Midwest)

It is clear from the experiences of these pastoral associates that a commitment to pastoral planning and visioning is a significant contribution to the vitality of parishes. These processes adapted from other organizational disciplines often contribute to the church's ability to be responsive to changing demographics, changing economics, and changing trends in local communities.

The changes that will occur are occurring so fast now that it is difficult to anticipate the future. There must be a change in leadership from a "structure" idea that takes time to react to, to a form that allows a process to

*develop for quick response to situations and events as
they occur. (Deacon, South)*

*We need to have processes to be "rangers" rather than
"garrisons." Rangers react quickly and are empowered
to make guidelines. The church structure needs to react
much quicker to what's happening. Solve sacramental
issues in two to four years, not in twenty years. (Pastoral
Leader, South)*

The practical optimism of pastoral leaders for the current and
future vitality of parish life is rooted, not only in a deep-seated,
faith-based commitment to the gospel, but also in a realistic
appraisal and understanding of their current circumstances.
In order to further digest, interpret, and discern priorities for
the future, these pastoral leaders appear well-grounded in the
disciplines of planning and visioning to assist in realizing their
core spiritual identity as vibrant eucharistic communities.

Figure 1
Importance of Pastoral Leadership Elements
(All Respondents)

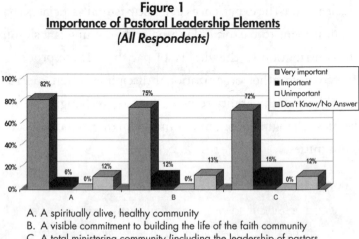

A. A spiritually alive, healthy community
B. A visible commitment to building the life of the faith community
C. A total ministering community (including the leadership of pastors,
   staff, and council together)

Figure 2
Effectiveness of Parish in Pastoral Leadership
(All Respondents)

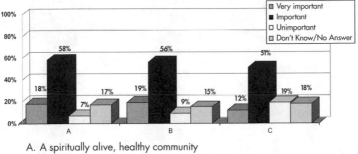

A. A spiritually alive, healthy community
B. A visible commitment to building the life of the faith community
C. A total ministering community (including the leadership of pastors, staff, and council together)

Figure 3
Confidence in Parish Becoming a Vibrtant Faith Community
(All Respondents)

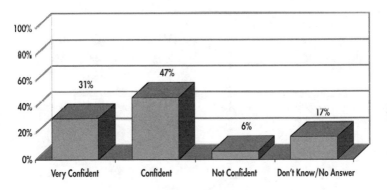

2

A Glimpse of the Future: Challenges and Opportunities

Symposia participants were asked to share their most personal and compelling leadership challenges and to identify any emerging opportunities for the future of their communities. While these participants do not represent a statistical sampling of pastoral leaders throughout the United States, the conversations of these diverse and recognized thought leaders provides a credible insight into how we look at, examine, and address the parish challenges of the future. These challenges included

- overcoming parochialism and resistance to change
- systemic and structural issues in church leadership
- emerging issues of theological, cultural, and multicultural diversity
- training and education for creating invitational and welcoming communities
- overcoming the dominant culture of self-centeredness and busyness

Overcoming Parochialism and Resistance to Change

Pastoral leaders repeatedly identified resistance to change as the most significant challenge they face in building vibrant faith communities for the future. One parish life coordinator from the North Central region stated it thus:

> *We are in a time of transition, and there is no experience on which parishioners can model a faith community. Our community looks different from the one they grew up in . . . fear of change is a challenge and there is a challenge in creating a shared vision. There is a need for a system and resources to form lay ecclesial leaders which now seems disjointed. (Parish Life Coordinator, North Central)*

The challenge of leading change was a common theme as pastoral leaders described numerous obstacles to forming multicultural communities, such as leading parishes without the active day-to-day presence of priests, the formation of laity, dealing with areas of economic decline, an aging Catholic population, and changing parish structures. For many of these pastoral leaders, dealing with change and the resistance they encounter is a constant in their day-to-day ministry.

> *No one has all the answers and all the gifts. Some are in ministries for too long . . . We need to accept change and continue conversion. We need to see who is missing and underserved in our communities. We need leaders to step back and take a fresh look . . . with a change of leadership and changing visions for a new generation, new challenges, new mentality, and different expectations (of the parish and church). (Pastor, Southwest)*

Systemic and Structural Issues in Church Leadership

Not surprisingly, these pastoral leaders reflected on the complex systemic and structural issues they face in pastoral leadership. Surprisingly, they focused very little time and energy on the sexual abuse scandals and financial challenges in the church. The structural issues they most often reflected upon included very practical day-to-day issues, including geographic distances of members in their communities, particularly in rural areas. They spoke of creating parishes with a sense of shared responsibility, of delegation, and of engaging laity in the life and mission of the church. They spoke candidly about the structural challenges of clearly and respectfully defining and living out roles for lay ecclesial leaders and priest-pastors in a way that combines their gifts for a common mission.

These pastoral leaders often spoke about the difficulties they face in establishing structures to train laity for future leadership roles and to develop a sense of service and mission as a consequence of one's baptismal call. One pastoral council member spoke of this challenge in the following way:

> The main challenges lie in a structure that prevents priests and other ministers from recognizing that they are first and foremost baptized. Everything else flows from that understanding. If ordained priesthood becomes understood as a way of living out one's baptismal commitment in service to the baptized, then the way in which authority is used can change and people might be able to enter into committed parish leadership knowing that the

work they do will not be undone by the next ordained
leader. (Pastoral Council Member, Southeast)

When faced with the difficult dynamic that places a theology of ordination over and against a theology of baptism, these pastoral leaders often articulated both fear and weariness in fulfilling the day-to-day needs of parish life. The challenge of reimagining a vision of shared leadership often leaves parishioners in a state of bewilderment and confusion.

> *Many Catholics are losing courage in the face of inse-*
> *curity and confusion arising from the changes that the*
> *church is attempting to make as it adapts its vision . . . to*
> *current times. There are significant numbers of very good*
> *people who simply want to return to a time when the*
> *destination and path seemed sure. They are willing to*
> *pay a high price for that return ticket. (Pastoral Associate,*
> *Southwest)*

Emerging Issues of Theological, Cultural, and Multicultural Diversity

Pastoral leaders seemed acutely aware of the complex challenges they face in forming and maintaining diverse yet viable faith communities in their parishes. It is interesting to note that they recognize not only multicultural diversity but also theological and economic diversity as well.

One pastoral leader from a large urban area of a major U.S. city indicated that twenty-seven different languages are spoken within her parish community which includes the poorest of the poor in that metropolitan area. Others spoke of the intense challenge of welcoming Hispanic members into their communities without adopting a dual parish model with one community meeting on Sunday morning and a separate Hispanic community meeting on Sunday afternoon and Sunday evening. One pastoral council member in the Southwest described the challenge this way:

> There are varying communities within the church with different customs and languages. How can leaders bring all those together without the melting pot conformity? We need to appreciate and learn about the other cultures. We need to be culturally aware without asking for change. We have faced these issues. Other communities are just beginning the process. There is a threat of "silo parishes" for multi-ethnicity. (Pastoral Council Member, Southwest)

Others spoke of their challenges with diversity in theological terms. They spoke of the struggle to avoid liberal and conservative stereotypes within the church, especially with regard to the role of women. A poignant moment in a symposium occurred when a young priest canon lawyer who was a self-identified conservative Catholic introduced a vowed religious woman as a trusted "co-pastor" of one of the southern parishes he oversees. She in turn surprised and dismayed many other participants as she expressed a reluctance to embrace the role of leading prayer as others had greater gifts in this area. Her concern was for the needs of the community, not her status as a parish life coordinator. No part of the imagery of this pastoral team fits neatly within a theological stereotype.

These pastoral leaders seem to have developed the skill of listening to the voices of many and respecting those voices by treating diversity as a rich and positive contribution to the life of the parish rather than as a threat to its viability. A priest from the Northeast summarized the importance of a respect for theological differences with this thought:

> Staff must be prepared to work with and for parishioners who might have very different theological viewpoints. We must get beyond our theological prejudices and realize that the spirit is within us when we are truly collaborative. (Pastor, Northeast)

Training and Education for Creating Invitational and Welcoming Communities

These pastoral leaders spoke eloquently about the challenges they face in creating communities with a true sense of outreach and invitation. Not surprisingly, these leaders in pastoral ministry spoke of the need to improve hospitality by training and educating people about the importance of creating hospitable communities as central to parish life. They spoke frequently of the need to educate people in the skills of communication, collaboration, and discernment. The educational challenges in ministry formation are particularly acute among those parishes that are located farther away from a local Catholic university or their diocesan center.

Pastoral leaders often spoke about the need for a formational process that empowers people with the awareness and skills necessary to realize their baptismal call to service. According to these leaders, dioceses are downsizing training programs or eliminating them all together due to economic necessity, at precisely the time when greater formation and training are needed for the laity in parishes. The unintended contradiction of these realities may have significant adverse consequences for the future viability of parishes.

Many pastoral leaders spoke of technology as a valuable resource for preparing laity for leadership roles and for nurturing their understanding of their baptismal call. Online courses and virtual learning communities may provide ways to develop leaders from diverse and remote communities with limited resources.

Pastoral leaders identified a host of issues to address in training laity for future parish leadership roles. These included the need to learn different languages, to develop team-building and collaboration skills, and to continue formation in spirituality and a sense of discipleship. The challenges they described are straightforward.

Overcoming the Dominant Culture of Self-centeredness and Busyness

These pastoral leaders described eloquently the challenges of the dominant culture in building vibrant faith communities. They often spoke of the demands and drains of cultural messages that reinforce individualism, materialism, and capitalism. One diocesan leader from the North Central region described the challenges this way:

> People's lives are so busy that they are unable to commit to serve. We live in such a mobile society that it creates difficulty in building a community of relationships. (Diocesan Representative, North Central)

Pastoral leaders also spoke about the attraction of mega-churches that appeal to people with a busy lifestyle by offer-ing forms of popular entertainment and a sense of immediate and intense community. Pastoral leaders often mentioned the need to strengthen parishes by utilizing technology for education and community formation. In addition, pastoral leaders expressed the importance of adapting to people's per-sonal needs, as many parishioners are often reluctant to give up family time or leave home because of the complexity of their lives.

The challenges of "busyness" and the demands of life are familiar, day-to-day companions of these pastoral leaders. As one pastoral associate from the Southeast expressed:

> How do we train and form leadership when they are so busy with their lives? Dual-income families leave little time to gather for involvement and training opportunities. The spirit is willing, but the logistics of reality are weak! (Pastoral Associate, Southeast)

At times, the challenges of pastoral engagement and pastoral imagination in addressing the complex needs of our culture seem at direct odds with the community context of a parish.

Opportunities and Hope

Pastoral leaders spoke, almost biblically, about their oppor-tunities to lead and build vibrant faith communities of the future. Despite the challenges and obstacles encountered, they exhibited an unmistakably grounded hope in the future of the parish.

The sky is the limit. The old paradigms are going away, so we must look for new ways. I think and pray often about the Acts of the Apostles. We are building a new church. The old way is passing away. There is a new church coming. (Pastor, Northeast)

The opportunities are endless in building the kingdom. Our work will never be finished. There will always be opportunities to deepen the faith of individuals and of a faith community. There will always be options to help the marginalized in our world. The opportunity to help people recognize, grow, and share their gifts in furthering God's kingdom and also to learn the ways in which these gifts are shared will strengthen the community and the faith life of individuals. (Pastoral Associate, Northeast)

Pastoral leaders in the symposia mentioned three dynamic ways they build vibrant faith communities. All reflect a very grassroots approach to engaging individuals and small groups in building the church. The following three strategies offer many opportunities for the future:

- calling forth the gifts of others
- ongoing formation and evangelization
- demonstrating the relevance of faith to the lives of people

Calling Forth the Gifts of Others

Pastoral leaders became intensely animated when they discussed their enthusiasm and fortitude in calling forth the gifts of people to build the kingdom in their local parishes. One diocesan representative expressed this well:

> Enable, invite, encourage all to be Christ for each other by participating in the mission, message, and ministry of Jesus; recognizing giftedness and calling it forth; reeducating the laity; calling people to participate in the life of the parish and community; mentoring new leaders who are invited to assume leadership roles for the future. (Diocesan Representative, South)

Pastoral leaders spoke frequently about processes, programs, and strategies that engage their communities in recognizing their baptismal call to service. Many of these programs demonstrate a sophisticated understanding, differentiating between ministries provided within the context of the parish and the discipleship of exercising leadership in the world. These pastoral leaders see many local and individualized opportunities to invite people to a greater sense of exercising their baptismal call to ministry.

> I believe with the growing awareness of our baptismal call to ministry, more people will come to realize the specific part they play in making the kingdom of God present in our time. With this implicitly comes the vibrancy of faith of those who know of their call to be part of the effort. (Parish Life Coordinator, Pacific Northwest)

Ongoing Formation and Evangelization

Pastoral leaders recognized that the key motivator for building vibrant faith communities is grounded in encouraging people to embrace their baptismal call to service and mission in the world. This recognition is further expressed as a desire to see an expansion of ongoing formation and evangelization efforts, animating the life of the church and the life of the larger culture through the vision of the church.

Formational efforts and evangelizing parishioners to reach out to others were named by participants as two key strategies for building vibrant communities.

> The people of God are more educated than ever. There are great team leadership possibilities with lay and clergy using gifts to serve communities. A new model of servant leadership is emerging. Opportunities to bridge a gap between lay and ordained are ever present. (Pastoral Associate, North Central)

Among their parishioners, pastoral leaders often encounter a thirst for knowledge and a desire to grow in faith. These leaders instinctively appear to identify and focus on the lay members of their communities who are ready for the next step in their spiritual challenge.

> The laity is much better educated. They are far more diverse than in the past which allows for greater opportunities to draw on a broader range of skill sets. There is a real hunger for participation in spiritual growth which can be tapped. If we are open to changes and willing to listen, there are far more options than challenges. (Deacon, Upper Midwest)

Pastoral leaders spoke about very practical tactics they use to respond to the spiritual hunger of those they serve. This intense effort of formation, catechesis, and evangelization in service to the church of the future appears to be a strategy taken straight from the Acts of the Apostles. One diocesan representative recommended the following to his colleagues:

> Improve methods of Pre-Cana and baptismal preparation. Bring willing leaders from the parish into church leadership. Be sensitive and thought provoking in homilies. Develop adult catechesis courses for laity, including pastoral studies in theology. Use laypeople for the training of Eucharist Ministers and Lectors, etc. Establish programs for laypeople run by laypeople with spiritual directors. (Diocesan Representative, Northeast)

These pastoral leaders did not reflect a naïve and unsophisticated sense of optimism for the formation of their communities, but rather a spiritual authenticity of recognizing that the gospel is communicated and developed one person and one community at a time.

> We must be authentic when dealing with others. In addition, we must seek out our brothers and sisters who have left us and encourage them to join us again. We also need to educate the laity on their responsibility as baptized Christians. (Pastor, Southeast)

Pastoral leaders spoke extensively about their ongoing formation programs: retreats, small Christian communities, whole community catechesis, missions, revivals, staff development, and pastoral plans. By various means and with the tools at hand, these pastoral leaders appear to rise above the cultural

challenges and structural demands of their ministry to provide ongoing formation, catechesis, and evangelization that
nurtures the next generation of leadership for our parishes.
One priest from the North Central United States expressed
his quiet confidence in the future:

> There is an enormous amount of opportunity for gather-
> ings, statistical analysis, education, and spiritual oppor-
> tunities to support and expand the horizons of those in
> leadership positions. This change and flux in society and
> the church is an opportunity as well. When you reach
> a point when it can't be done as before, it creates the
> opportunity to do something new and creative. (Pastor,
> North Central)

Demonstrating the Relevance of Faith to the Lives of People

Pastoral leaders in the regional symposia described their roles
clearly as ambassadors of grace. They know very well that the
root of faith is established by demonstrating its relevance in
the lives of people. Consequently, they are intentional in their
actions and words as they invite people to reflect on faith as a
day-to-day living reality.

> The need for Christian Catholic values is ever more appar-
> ent. People long for a meaningful connection to community
> and a spiritually meaningful life. (Pastor, Upper Midwest)

These pastoral leaders are often very sophisticated in their
approach to blending psychological and business studies with
their animation in faith. They have learned to incorporate and

adapt the knowledge of their cultures into the formation of communities in order to make faith ever more relevant in the lives of their parishioners.

> Disciplines like psychology in business have studied organizational leadership that can be adapted to faith communities. The culture creates an atmosphere in which communities based in hope are attractive and a community whose mission is to transform the world gives meaning to life. We need to tell the Catholic story. (Parish Life Coordinator, Northwest)

Pastoral leaders are exceedingly intentional in their efforts to educate and inform people about the word of God at hand. They recognize the inherent hunger of the gospel despite the layers of obstacles in our current Western culture. They appear resilient in the way they connect people to faith on a very personal level and bring greater relevance to their lives. A pastoral associate from the Upper Midwest spoke of it this way:

> An increasingly educated laity that is ready to take responsibility for the powers they have and use them for the reign of God is the best way they can discover faith. They . . . are especially interested in viewing their work lives as a contribution to God's reign. In the areas of pastoral ministry, my work with university people assures me that there are enough young people willing to do professional pastoring in its various forms if they are simply given a welcome into the profession, a reasonable wage, and a path for advancement as their ability and

experience grow with reasonable job security. (Pastoral Associate, Upper Midwest)

Pastoral leaders spoke about their ability to call people beyond their day-to-day challenges in life to explore the gospel and its call to their mission and ministry in the world. They appear to have an innate sensitivity to the hunger they find around them despite the sometimes formidable obstacles of finance, attendance, shifting demographics, and changing economic conditions in their communities. Perhaps through the maturity of their faith they see beyond the myriad of changes and move toward a hunger for the gospel they encounter in their midst. One priest from the Southwest spoke of his journey:

> *People are hungry for the gospel. The numbers attending church are increasing. You don't have to travel the path alone if you look around. The spirit provides in every faith community what it needs. We just have to acknowledge it. (Pastor, Southwest)*

Despite the seemingly endless obstacles and challenges these pastoral leaders face, they seem to exhibit a biblical sense of how to nurture their faith traditions by working with those among them in parish life. They were repeatedly animated in their descriptions of calling forth the gifts of others, their efforts in formation and evangelization, and their commitment to make faith increasingly relevant to the lives of their parishioners. Can the gospel be in any better hands than these courageous optimists?

3

Emerging Parish Structures

Pastoral leaders from the Emerging Models Regional Symposia represented diverse parish experiences. Rural parish leaders recounted experiences of parishes more than one hundred miles away from their next closest parish community led by a council of laypeople with a pastor whose visits are weeks apart. Rural parishes also can find themselves caring for large populations of migrant farmworkers. Urban communities included parishes in suburban and exurban areas with diverse pastoral staff, including multiple clergy, deacons, and lay professionals providing leadership to vast congregations, in some cases exceeding 6,000 households. Other urban settings represented poor inner cities with a single pastoral leader serving an entire urban parish community with parishioners from more than a dozen ethnic heritages. Consequently, the views of these diverse pastoral leaders on future emerging parish structures were highly instructive.

Parish structures cited by symposia participants varied according to local conditions, which included the following:

- economics of the local community
- geography as an urban, rural, or suburban community
- demographics, including the racial and ethnic composition of their surrounding civic communities

The diversity of parish leadership structures is reflected by the uniqueness of the circumstances in which pastoral leaders find themselves. While we expected to find some established and systematic patterns of emerging parish leadership structures, we found instead a wide range of parish structures designed to meet the unique needs of local communities. In a break from the history of parishes in this country, no single definition of parish leadership seemed more predictive of the future. Leaders described the following models:

- traditional priest/pastor-centered parishes
- collaborative pastoral teams, pastoral councils, and ministry oversight through lay planning boards
- parish life coordinators with regular presence of priests/ pastors for Eucharist
- parish life coordinators with infrequent priest/pastor presence (especially among the rural or urban poor)
- clustered and merged parishes with nominal integration of ministries
- clustered parishes with distinct identities served by fully integrated pastoral teams and/or shared ministries
- megaparishes with distributed leadership groups for lay coordination of ministries
- parishioner-led parishes

Pastoral leaders in the symposia were asked what parish structures they expect to emerge during the next twenty years of parish life. Though their viewpoints, not surprisingly, were influenced by their current local experiences, several emerging themes appeared in their reflections and written observations.

On a whole, these pastoral leaders expect parish structures of the future to have the following characteristics:

- to be grounded in a local faith community and in the discernment of local needs
- to participate in a regional community of communities
- to include emerging faith-based networks that are cross-parochial and transcend local parish structures
- to include megachurches
- to utilize small intentional faith communities as a building block for the future
- to represent an evolving process of emerging redefinitions with numerous challenges and opportunities

Grounded in a Local Faith Community and in the Discernment of Local Needs

Pastoral leaders often described the emerging local church as a process of discerning local needs, grounded in the faith-based reflection of parishioners, local leaders, and diocesan officials on the preferred identity and structure of the local church. Clearly, these pastoral leaders anticipate a future where the structural form of the local church will enjoy far more diversity than currently exists. They cited many factors contributing to this situation-based definition of parish structures, including the diminished availability of ordained clergy and greater awareness among the laity of the baptismal call to service.

These pastoral leaders often described an era of experimentation within their local parishes and dioceses to determine the most suitable structures. The common element of this process is a spirit of faith-based discernment that leads a local community and its supporting diocese in developing a structural approach tailored to the local circumstances. This, in and of itself, is a shift in practice.

> More people in the parish community are coming to realize that the changes in the "church" as a whole are affecting how a church community will function because of the difficulties in leadership and, therefore, are becoming more curious and maybe more willing to "step up to the plate and go to bat" for the parish community. (Pastoral Council Member, Northeast)

> Our diocese is using different models (yoked parishes and pastoral leaders). Our parish is in a growing, one-church town. It is likely our model will stay the same (one priest, one parish) as long as the priest supply permits. Our issue or change opportunity for the future is to formalize our volunteer structure, clarify our purpose, and build our talents and services. (Pastoral Council Member, Northeast)

> We're experimenting with charism discernment for the whole community, using a formal instrument developed by the Catherine of Siena Institute. We're also beginning to encourage some of our stronger programs and activities, if they are not part of our core mission, to become independent of our structure and self-sufficient. (Pastor, Pacific Northwest)

> When there are different cultures in a parish, one model of ministry may not work within those cultural groups.

The priest is looked upon in many of our cultural com-
munities as the leader. If this is to shift to having a PLC,
much catechesis needs to be done before a different
model of leadership is introduced. With the shortage
of priests, I'm seeing the priest more as a sacramental
minister. For some priests, they would welcome this and
not be worried about administrative duties. (Diocesan
Representative, Southwest)

Regional Community of Communities

A consistent expectation among symposia participants is that
the local church of the future will extend beyond any individual local parish and have far more of a regional identity.
This image of a community of communities best captures
their expected reality. Many described this regional church
as a network of local parishes, envisioned as clusters. Others
foresaw a more integrated set of regional ministries that serve
member parishes.

A variety of experiments and experiences appears to be
underway among their parish communities, often sponsored
and supported by their local dioceses. Clearly, a much more pervasive regional definition of the parish community is expected
among these pastoral leaders throughout the United States.

The statements below describe some ways in which pastoral leaders are creating this regional or clustered identity
of the local church. This regional perspective of the local
church is also similar to the radical change experienced by
various not-for-profit and community-based organizations
throughout the United States when faced with the redefinition of their local communities and outreach. Parishes

and pastoral leaders are far more inclined to focus on their regional geographic communities for common ministries, shared resources, and shared staff. The growing number of vicariate and deanery plans within dioceses appears to be substantial. The trend to linking parishes and multiple-parish pastoring is an example of this.[5] Here are some reflections on this regional Catholic identity:

> We are putting into place a deanery council that will be linked in purpose to all of our parish pastoral councils. It is my hope that such councils will develop an "internal dynamic" much like that of a neighborhood association, since many of our members energetically want to be Catholic, want to remain in the community rather than move, and want our values of faith to make a difference in the community. (Pastor, North Central)

> We are stabilizing our present situation, but in the future, I see we might move to clustered or megachurches with trying to return to small Christian communities or other models of praying and reflecting during the week and gathering together for Sunday worship. (Pastoral Associate, Northeast)

> Now we are a cluster of five parishes. I am not sure if the cluster is activated to make and implement a pastoral plan. I believe that the five parishes have currently four pastors. I assume a plan for fewer clergy will need to be developed. I am not sure what it will eventually look like as far as a model is concerned. (Pastoral Leader, Northeast)

Our future model would be a cluster of two parishes—a pastor of one would be the canonical pastor of another. There would be a pastoral coordinator over the one who would be responsible for all the aspects of the parishes. This is already the case in parishes in the diocese. Another model of the future would be more of a team ministry; this could become a reality this year. (Diocesan Representative, Southeast)

Our diocesan plan is "Area Faith Communities," a number of parishes with one parish pastoral council (individual finance councils) and some form of shared ministerial staff. This model is just beginning. (Pastor, North Central)

Emergence of Cross-Parochial Faith-Based Networks

A number of pastoral leaders described cross-parochial faith-based networks as ways to organize the local church in the future. Most of these networks are supplemental to the local parishes; however, they represent ways to engage specific populations of people, especially young adults and people of diverse cultural backgrounds. As an organizing principle, these "networks of faith" represent an interesting way to connect parish communities and regional churches in the future. Nearly all the descriptions of young adult ministry shared during the symposia process mentioned the importance of engaging youth in their faith lives through peer group networks that transcend parish-centric boundaries. The following statements summarize how pastoral leaders are experiencing this limited, but interesting, phenomenon of specialized groupings of communities of faith:

The Hispanic young adult group is emerging as a network that operates within the parish, but is unified as a body of groups on the diocesan level. These groups develop their own leadership teams that work closely with me, but direct their group catechetical plan according to the method they feel will work best with their peers. The leadership takes the initiative to be formed by diocesan efforts as well. This group is a model of a lay group which takes responsibility for ongoing evangelization for both the leaders themselves and the members of the group. The fact that these young adults also build up a larger network within the diocese enables collaboration, common retreats, sharing of resources, formation, etc. This model may work for all young adult ministries, if done well. (Pastoral Leader, South)

We worked on a nonparochial approach to create communities of faith (clusters) consisting of several parishes where talents and resources were shared. We took inspiration from Acts 2:44—"They shared their goods in common"—and from the maxim "United We Stand, Divided We Fall." Don't do separately what you can do better together. (Pastor, Northeast)

I think there is some wisdom to the idea of intentional communities—gathered around a facet of church that excites a group of people (e.g., social justice/outreach). I also think the exciting place to look for signs will be the parishes farthest from the chancery. There will need to be experimentation and creativity. The parish will be much more inclusive. (Deacon, Upper Midwest)

Megachurches

Pastoral leaders in the symposia process often referenced megachurches as an expected emerging model. Not surprisingly, many pastoral leaders spoke of megachurches as "a necessary, but less desirable," image of the local church in the future. In nearly all instances, these pastoral leaders see the megachurch as a community of communities.

The megachurch phenomenon in the United States is most prevalent and popular among evangelical communities. This structure, however, may be more difficult for traditional mainline churches to embrace, including Catholic communities. Nonetheless, megachurches are perceived as an expected organizing practice for the local church of the next twenty years. Pastoral leaders spoke of their mega-church expectations and experiences with a muted sense of enthusiasm. Many pastoral leaders were ambivalent about this form of the local church, which they perceive to be an inevitable reality.

> Many will be larger in size due to geographic consolidations necessitating smaller groups organized by neighborhood, apostolate, and spiritual interests. Parish staffs will be larger, composed mainly of the pastor and a team that will have responsibilities for coordinating and facilitating the work of committees. (Deacon, South)

> Parishes inevitably will be bigger. Ways will be found to divide these larger parishes into multiple units. Sunday Masses will be made up of many subcommunities comprising one large worshipping community. (Pastor, South)

Megastyle will exist only because of the lack of priestly vocations. This would not be a natural emerging model if we had sufficient vocations. Lay leaders are the life-blood of parish life. However, parishes will be much larger in the future, much less personable in the worship setting. Best practices are much more difficult (if not impossible) to achieve in this style of parish. (Diocesan Representative, South)

Large centers for Sunday worship strategically located in dioceses. Present churches will function as chapels for small faith communities where weddings and funerals may take place. Few places with resident priests; more priests will live in common and travel to parishes for ministry. (Diocesan Representative, Southeast)

Consolidation of parishes—megaparishes in the large metropolitan centers—strong commitment to ESL (English as a second language) programs to promote integration and assimilation of the laity. (Pastoral Leader, Southeast)

There will be some megachurches with emphasis on small Christian communities in large growing cities; more frequently clusters of small parish communities with resident lay pastoral administrators and priest guidance. (Pastoral Leader, South)

Small Intentional Faith Communities

A nearly universal expectation of symposia participants included small intentional faith-based communities as a basic element of organizing the local church. Whether the parish of the future is included in a regional cluster of churches or in a megachurch, in small rural communities or in larger suburban areas, the small intentional faith community appears to be a central expectation for organizing faith-based communities of the future.

Many pastoral leaders believe these smaller faith communities will provide a substantive opportunity for a supportive parish to nurture the faith of their members. Others believe that the small faith-based community offers the best opportunity for whole community catechesis in the faith formation of adults as well as children. Yet other pastoral leaders see these small faith communities as ways to contribute to a specific outreach or ministry, such as a social justice ministry.

Some pastoral leaders find that small faith-based communities offer a sense of dichotomy or tension with the local parish. They wonder how these communities will thrive and flourish with the diminished availability of the eucharistic life of a larger parish. To the extent that the future of parishes will involve less frequent celebrations of the Eucharist, further fragmentation of the identity of the parish into small faith-based communities represents a substantial challenge to parish life. Some pastoral leaders expect the small intentional community to replace the structures of the parish church.

Despite the diversity of expectations and differences in demographics, pastoral leaders in the symposia appear to agree that small faith-based communities offer an opportunity for a vibrant center that nurtures the life of Catholics and builds their sense of discipleship for the future.

*Small group spiritual gatherings will occur with an empha-
sis on conversion. Model of intergenerational spirituality
where there is openness to the members of our community, which will help see God in his workings through all
generations. (Pastor, Northeast)*

*Small faith communities are an important part of the par-
ish. Parish leadership is emerging from these groups.
(Pastor, South)*

*Small faith-sharing groups (several are going very well).
More efforts to be justice-focused, as well as charitable.
Women in professional ministry roles are working to
teach the community about lay ecclesial ministry (it's not
easy!). (Pastoral Associate, North Central)*

*A family church with small communities; whole community
catechesis; deacon-led or lay-led communion services;
Sunday celebration in the absence of a priest; intentional
eucharistic communities; area churches in halls, community centers, etc. (Deacon, Southwest)*

*Small Christian communities are forming as faith-sharing
groups, Bible studies, households are meeting off campus, and leaders are emerging from these small groups.
(Pastoral Leader, Southwest)*

*I don't think all the parishes of the future will look the same.
There will be many different models of parish. Hopefully,
most will have strong lay leadership, small faith communities, and have vibrant celebrations of the Eucharist that will*

be the center of life and transform the community into true disciples of Jesus. (Diocesan Representative, Mid-Atlantic)

Perhaps smaller, but with more commitment on the part of those who remain. To always be concerned with inviting and evangelizing intentionally. The parish will need to be a place that brings disciples to serve in the marketplace. (Pastor, North Central)

Faith will be lived in small faith communities that interact with other faith traditions to make a positive difference in the world. The layperson's role will move from dependent to independent—from childish to adult living of the faith. The parish of the future will be less priest-focused— though the priest will always be a valued person. (Parish Life Coordinator, North Central)

The parish of the future won't be territorial or boundary driven. It will be a place for people of faith to gather and celebrate union, communion, support, prayer, and a connection with the transcendent and eminent relationship of Christ, Our Savior. It will be faith-based, small communities that can't live in this world without it. (Pastor, Northeast)

A Process of Emerging Challenges and Opportunities

As the local parish has for centuries been the foundation of local communities and faith life, it is easy to anticipate a long journey to determine local church structures of the future.

Many believe that the precipitating factor when considering alternate structures for the local church is the diminished availability of clergy to serve as resident pastors. However, looking at the larger cultural and cross-cultural trends among many forms of local civic, neighborhood, school, service, and parochial communities, nearly all types of communities are reexamining their future forms and structures.

Local governments are looking at alternative ways to cooperate and merge with neighboring cities, townships, and counties. Large and small not-for-profit organizations are looking to evaluate new economies of scale which in many cases foreshadow greater consolidation and increased regionalism in their forms and identities.

Many universities have abandoned traditional geographic recruitment areas and are using the Internet and online education as a global means of recruiting and educating students. Many of these challenges, including demographics and economics, face the local church in the United States. It may be simplistic to think that the structural challenges facing our church are driven simply by the experience of diminished availability of clergy to serve as resident pastors.

Our local structures and basic organizing principles are not exempt from those larger cultural forces that shape organizational identities and structures and define the forms of local communities. Clearly, the pastoral leaders in the symposia process expect many decades of experimentation and transformation in determining those new and emerging forms of organizing the local church. As parishes, dioceses, and pastoral leaders embrace this uncertain future, their efforts might be better grounded in optimism and exploration rather than in resistance and frustration. We may be content with finding the *next*-best answer to local situations rather than a definitive answer to what the parish of the future will look like.

The pastoral leaders who participated in the symposia process gave us a glimpse of an optimistic, yet undetermined, sense of the future when anticipating the most appropriate parochial structures to organize the local church. Some may see in these challenges a diminishment and perhaps a loss of a local parish identity. Others see this as a period of imagination where the opportunity for rebirth, redefinition, and revitalization of community life is ever possible. The following views represent a range of optimism for the redefinition of the parish:

> In a rural community, I foresee a partnering of parishes in order to support and share resources. If intentional effort is not made to foster and nourish Catholic identity, then I foresee people turning to other alternatives and a parish may no longer exist. I wonder how the dichotomy of communal and sacramental life will adversely affect parishes and perhaps be the deciding factor to close a parish. (Pastoral Leader, North Central)

> I hope the parish of the future will be smaller with its emphasis on supporting the work of its members in the world beyond the parish plant. I hope that it is a community of people who feel a common task with God and with one another to bring the world to the promise God has filled it with from the beginning. (Pastoral Associate, Upper Midwest)

I hope the community will be "life-now focused" rather than "life-hereafter focused." I hope the community will be much more "life-for-all focused" rather than "life-for-me-and-mine focused." I hope that the pastoral ministers and the parish as a whole will view pastoral ministry as simply carrying out that part of the parish's activity that must be devoted to parish maintenance so that the rest of the parish can succeed in its work for the larger world. I hope the whole parish, pastoral personnel included, will move beyond the idea that roles in life are gender determined. I hope that the priestly function that is given to each person at baptism will be seen as exercised, but not exhausted, by the ministry of the ordained . . . I hope that the ordained will come to see themselves as part of a work being carried out by the spirit of God through the entire parish that is much bigger than themselves and their ritual activities. I hope that all the parish will understand the cross not as something that Jesus endured on behalf of people, but something that Jesus endured to free people to accept their own crosses as they become inevitable in the pursuit of God's reign. (Pastoral Associate, Upper Midwest)

II
VISIBLE COMMITMENT
TO BUILDING THE LIFE
OF THE PARISH

4

Ministries of Word, Worship, and Service

Symposia participants were asked, in a futuring exercise, where they believed the ministries of the parish were headed. This highly energizing exercise led participants to a sense of realism about the impact of changing trends on parish life and leadership. Their responses indicate a strong sense of the call of all the baptized to discipleship and the increased role parishioners will play in the life of the parish. With great creativity they spoke of ways to adapt to today's reality and named the growing need to prepare faith communities for increased lay leadership and responsibilities, especially in ministries of word, worship, and service.

Future Ministries of the Word

Ministries of the word have been carried by parishioners for many years. Pastoral leaders not only see this continuing but increasing in scope, as parishioners take on greater roles in today's parishes. Young adults are asking for more formation in their faith. Parishioners are seeking formation for the various ministries they are taking on within the parish community and beyond. With the linking of parishes and the formation of megaparishes, parishioners are recognizing they must support and help form one another. These thoughts are expressed in the following response of one pastoral council member when asked about the future of ministry of the word:

Internet-based; deeper spirituality—formation by laity— faith-sharing communities; generations of faith-community catechesis; environmental movement with Scripture; commitment; welcoming; multicultural faith sharing; interfaith generation understanding; Catholics will or should be more comfortable with the Bible. Up close and personal media stewardship of the earth. The word needs to speak to the signs of the time. (Pastoral Council Representative, Northeast)

Increased opportunities for adult formation, especially preaching

Participants identified adult formation as a prime area for development, especially through biblical studies. These new forms of catechesis will be Gospel based, multilingual, and multigenerational.

Symposia participants believe that lay catechists will be much more involved in proclaiming the word by leading worship in the future, especially in offering reflections at non-eucharistic services. Formation is needed for this ministry. Many expect that certification programs will emerge to prepare laity for this role in teaching and preaching the word.

Leaders of faith sharing around the word will be trained in Scripture interpretation and prayer leadership. Catechesis will become more prominent as a foundation for the faith, and it will extend to all stages of life. The faith will be sustained by the word and celebrated in the Eucharist. (Pastor, Mid-Atlantic)

More biblical studies and whole-community catechesis

Many parish communities are relying on whole-community catechesis. They are recognizing that with limited time and the challenges of today's world, communities benefit from learning together. Whether referring to packaged programs or creating their own, many communities are excited about this approach to formation.

Multicultural ministries of the word

Some of the greatest challenges, however, come in providing catechesis to parishes of increasing cultural and ethnic diversity. Parishes must decide whether to combine programs or offer separate tracks and are recognizing the need to find creative responses. This is especially poignant in youth groups where teens enjoy time together across cultures but still have very specific needs that are addressed solely in their native language and cultural understanding.

Technology, Internet, and media

Participants are well aware that technology will play a greater role in the development of educational resources for catechesis. Catechetical program publishers are taking advantage of this trend in packaging their programs, especially for children and teens. Parishes must also make use of modern technologies such as multimedia presentations, computers, iPods, and the Internet. These will be especially effective in evangelization and proclamation. For example, some priests are recording their homilies for podcasting. Colleges are recording classroom presentations to make them available via distance learning—university-based online catechetical programs. In a world where young adults will need to be evangelized in ways their parents did not, parishes will find the use of Internet technologies an especially helpful tool.

Formation for care of the planet

Also evident was a strong and urgent awareness of another area of formation for the future, namely, the care for the planet and those most affected by climate change.

Future of Ministries of Worship

Symposia participants anticipate changes in ministries of worship. More leadership of worship will be given to the laity because of the diminishing number of ordained available to provide regular eucharistic liturgies. Additionally, the preferences of the next generation and of those who bring a differing cultural awareness to prayer will impact the future.

> *Eucharist will remain the center, but the faith will be sustained by the Liturgy of the Hours and Scripture sharing as the frequency of eucharistic celebrations will decrease. (Pastor, Mid-Atlantic)*

Diverse forms of worship

In a time when easy access to eucharistic liturgies is ebbing, participants recognize that more diverse forms of worship will be necessary. Pastors see a future in which eucharistic liturgies will be celebrated no more than weekly, perhaps even monthly; at the very least they will be celebrated in megachurches that can accommodate more people and fewer masses. Pastors also believe it is possible that sacraments such as penance or matrimony will be incorporated into regular weekend liturgies. They believe worship experiences will be varied and adapted to the style of individual communities. There will be greater emphasis on non-eucharistic liturgies, such as the Liturgy of the Word, the Liturgy of the Hours, and Taizé-style prayers and adoration.

Pastoral leaders were deeply concerned about a future parish life with limited access to the eucharistic celebration. Many expressed the view that limited access to the Eucharist would diminish the very Catholic identity and nature of the parish and parish members. Participants believed that a regular eucharistic liturgy is essential to the vitality and definition of the parish. Notably, participants did not foresee greater use of *Sunday Celebrations in the Absence of a Priest*. Participants were unwavering in their insistence on Eucharist as essential and expected that other forms of ministry would evolve to accommodate it. Others feel that after some experimentation there will be a return to the sense that Eucharist is about the gathered community.

> *Much more emphasis on careful liturgical planning. After some experimentation with a few electronic additions such as worship aids, the emphasis will return to the gathering experiences and the specific nature of Catholic worship. (Pastor, South)*

Multicultural worship

Above all, participants expect worship in the future to be decidedly more multicultural in expression, including devotions that are unique to a variety of individual, ethnic, and cultural groups.

> *More multicultural and multilingual; Liturgy of the Hours; communion and word services; and Scripture study in small faith groups. (Parish Life Coordinator, South)*

Increased role of the laity

Participants also anticipate less access to the Eucharist with more reliance on paraliturgical and communion services. These changes will allow for the laity to play an increased role in leading worship, possibly even preaching and witnessing to the word. Many see the need for preaching by the laity, especially in appropriate non-eucharistic settings. Not only will the forms and leadership of worship vary, so too will the presentation. Participants believe there will be greater emphasis on improved preaching, music, and technology. Non-eucharistic liturgies will provide the possibility for more creativity in developing forms of worship.

Deeper commitment, appreciation, and ownership of worship

Responses from participants revealed a deep appreciation of worship and prayer as essential to the future of parish life. They believe that there will be a deeper commitment, appreciation, and ownership of worship by parish members. With less access to the Eucharist there will be a greater appreciation for the sacraments and eucharistic devotional practices. Formation of adults to preside in this emerging reality, along with a deepening of biblical formation, will become the norm.

Future Ministries of Service

Participants believe that a greater understanding of Catholic social teaching, including its service to the poor and marginalized, will be crucial to the success of ministries of service now emerging to meet the growing needs of the world. They believe there will be an expansion of outreach services, especially social justice ministries to the poor and marginalized.

More emphasis on social justice and catholic social teaching

There was a strong sense that cutbacks in government and social agencies will force religious organizations to step forward and respond to circumstances in society that governments and other institutions can no longer address. People will turn to churches to meet their financial as well as spiritual needs. Churches will begin recognizing that we are called to meet global as well as local needs. In the process, Catholic social teaching will have a greater political impact.

> *Respect for life and its quality; care for the elderly in churches and the homebound; have doctors and nurses of parish help; creative solutions; prison visits—help them in transition out of prison; feed the hungry; help those addicted to anything; collaboration of parish and young adults to join in. (Parishioner, Northeast)*

In addition to changes in our world, participants recognize that changing circumstances of parish life and leadership are calling for a paradigm shift in how ministries of service are delivered.

> The perception that Father or Sister is in the church to do the ministries of service has already been dealt a blow. With some reluctance the laity at large are stepping forward, but in the future, it will be impelling that the level of awareness and demand of gospel service be realized in the individual lives of the community. (Lay Minister, Southeast)

More collaborative and ecumenical approach to intentional service

One of the hallmarks of the pastoral leaders we met was their understanding of social justice and service along with their ability to incorporate it into their ministry. We have come to understand the value of Catholic social teaching and the call to serve the poor. As seen in the ministries of word and worship, service is also an area of ministry in which the laity have played a significant role for some time.

Increased role of service as part of parish identity

Justice and service play an essential role in parish life. Participants saw the role of service increasing, defining the overall identity of the parish and essential to its mission. Reemergence of social justice and Catholic social teaching will be a prevalent trend for the future of parish ministries. Participants express this in a variety of ways, including a greater concern and respect for the quality of life. They stress an emerging intentionality of justice ministries as part of the fabric of faith communities. In areas and issues such as housing, mental health, child protection services, or the right to life, parishioners are being called to respond to needs in their parish and civic community.

Participants clearly believe that the future of parishes and the church as a whole will be strengthened by their commitment and ability to engage people to realize their baptismal call to ministry. They are realistic about the implications of a church that depends on ordained men to provide Eucharist, and the implications of a growing cultural shift in parishes. At the same time they seek the emergence of new forms of ministry, not just as a paradigmatic response to a shortage of clergy, but as a new opportunity for the church to realize the full participation of its members in the mission of the gospel with the church and in the world.

5

Spirituality of Parish Life

The Emerging Models Project asked lay and ordained leaders to talk about parish life, listening deeply to what these ministers said and to the *language* they chose to describe their reality and hopes for their parishes. From their collective sharing a portrait of an implicit, operative ecclesiology of parish began to emerge. Though deeply rooted in the central event of Eucharist, this is more than a sacramental ecclesiology. These ministers' understanding of parish extends beyond the mere gathering of a people, beyond a simple yet constitutive sense of community to one that has been called, initiated, and sent, and is inclusive of all God's people.

Pastoral leaders were asked, "What makes a parish spiritually vital and alive?" Over and over, in one form or another, the answer came back: that they are *welcoming eucharistic communities.* Contained in their responses are implications for an ecclesiology of parish, described by one participant in the following words:

> *I believe the spirituality of the community begins with prayer, especially the Eucharist. Celebrating good liturgy, good preaching, and good faith sharing will only deepen the community's spirituality. From that prayer comes a healthy community. (Diocesan Representative, Southwest)*

Pastoral leaders express an understanding of parish as

- an inclusive community of believers
- rooted in the dynamic mystery of Eucharist
- comprised of members called by baptism
- support oriented
- served by designated pastoral leaders
- sent out into the world

This operative theology of parish has three major components: communion, inclusion, and Eucharist.

Communion and Mission

When pastoral leaders talk about "community" they have incorporated the Vatican II understanding of the church as the people of God. Their responses were concrete and pragmatic indicating that the parish as the visible gathering of the Body of Christ has become constitutive of their understanding. Pastoral leaders in the symposia were consistent in their descriptions of community vitality reflecting both formational and action-oriented dimensions.

> The Council of Ministries, the pastor, the professional lay staff, the six commissions, and the many ministries are all linked together, each sharing a role in our common mission as church. Through these structures, we call forth and form a community of disciples who then go forth as signs of God's presence in the world. (Parish Life Coordinator, South)

> We acknowledge the scope of spiritualities in the community. We are a lectionary-based community putting

the word of God into daily life and rediscovering the baptismal commitment. Assembly is fully active and conscious in their participation. (Pastor, Southwest)

The Holy Spirit is definitely at work—people are taking their roles in the parish more seriously, embracing discipleship and deepening their understanding of their baptism—and they are being empowered. (Pastoral Associate, Mid-Atlantic)

A study of parishes conducted for the Project by the National Pastoral Life Center made clear that vibrant and alive parishes have a great deal going on. They have vibrant liturgies, engaged staffs, significant programming, and active parishioners. Pastoral leaders expressed an understanding of community as *communio*, reflecting a vision of the parish as comprising those initiated into the community, focused on the Eucharist, and lived out in discipleship.

My parish is vibrant, spiritually alive and healthy. There are over 100 organizations and 155 meetings a month, 3 priests, 3 religious, 75 full-time employees, a school of over 900, a CCD of over 800, perpetual adoration, etc. (Pastor, North Central)

Both of my small parishes (400 households and 150 households) are vibrant and viable faith communities. They have active religious education programs, RCIA, and strong youth ministry. My parish has 310 students— preschool to 12th grade (over 70 students in grades 9–12). Yes, they come to RE after confirmation. The pastoral councils seem to understand their role of vision-ing for the future. Liturgies are alive and faith filled. Father preaches in a way that I believe upholds the spirituality of the people. (Parish Life Coordinator, North Central)

Our parish community has an intergenerational faith-formation program, hundreds of laypeople involved in ministries, such as BeFrienders, eucharistic ministers, social justice and advocacy, a pastor who believes in empower-ing staff and laypeople alike to "vision" for the church. We have a pastor who challenges all of us to truly witness our baptism. (Diocesan Representative, North Central)

We are on the road to becoming spiritually alive, but I believe we are striving to live the gospel out in the world. Are we healthy? Well, in many ways, we are the sticky-gooey church with its inherent dysfunction. But we are moving toward wholeness and work toward expression of and recognition of all different spiritualities. (Pastoral Associate, Southwest)

Sunday Eucharist is a powerful, spirit-filled celebration made more meaningful by the expression of faith and joy in the midst of great poverty. Monday nights are reserved for prayer. Friday nights are "family nights." No meetings may be held on Monday or Friday. Every two months the community gathers for a healing prayer service. And at least once a month we celebrate a bilingual (English-Spanish) liturgy which unites the entire parish around the table of the Lord. (Pastor, Mid-Atlantic)

Strong; warm; welcoming; strong active parish advisory board; meaningful, uplifting liturgies; strong, creative liturgy committee; sacramental programs; baptism prep team; marriage prep team (Pre-Cana); parish retreats; parish missions; adult catechesis and Scripture study groups; pastor warm, pastoral, compassionate. Would not ask you to do anything he himself does not do. He walks the walk. (Pastoral Associate, Mid-Atlantic)

Inclusion

"Welcoming the stranger" has become one of the great challenges of U.S. parishes. Catholic parishes are called to welcome all genders, generations, and ideologies; the poor; the handicapped; and the elderly. They are challenged to welcome those of multiple cultural and ethnic backgrounds as they arrive with their differing spiritual needs. There is a particular call to understand the church in the United States as a multicultural reality, transcending "at once all times and all boundaries between peoples" (LG 9).

Respondents' understanding of parish appears to be defined, not only by the community that is gathered, but also by *how* the community is gathered. Spiritually alive parishes are described as welcoming communities, and when people talked about being "welcoming" they were not just talking about having greeters and hospitality committees. They were using the language of inclusion found in the church's Judeo-Christian tradition.

The spirit is evident in the faces and numbers of people and families who gather to worship and celebrate. The people . . . young and old reflect faith alive and healthy in their faces and the joy and concern in how they welcome and greet each other. (Pastor, Mid-Atlantic)

Being open to the youth as the church of today; attention to one's spiritual, relational, and physical self; being the prophetic voice of the poor, marginalized in affluent communities; asking the question to all decisions, "How will this affect all people of all economic and social levels?" Welcoming diversity. (Pastoral Associate, Upper Midwest)

Some signs: welcoming atmosphere, strong lay involvement, sense of community, awareness of connection to global community, diverse ministry groups, conscious of multigenerational profile, etc. (Diocesan Representative, Pacific Northwest)

Bridging the gap between the sections of the individual congregations; getting the section of parishioners content with celebrating the Eucharist to "transform" and become truly active members living out Christ's mission of loving one another in all that we do. Reaching out to the Hispanic community and truly welcoming them to be an integral part of the whole community. (Pastoral Leader, Southeast)

We are spiritually alive and healthy based on these facts. New building in progress, Sunday Mass is bilingual, our cultures merge well, and a new generation is stepping into the spotlight of parish life. (Pastoral Leader, South)

Eucharist

We are eucharistic communities. We are a sacramental people. This identity pervades our imagination, our speech, and our interpretation and understanding of leadership. We are a eucharistic people. This is core to the identity of pastoral leaders. Project participants are dedicated, faith-filled leaders whose ministry is focused and centered on the Eucharist. Their expressions of heartfelt longing are often spontaneous and intense. The desire most often expressed is for accessible and available eucharistic celebrations in small, faith-filled communities. What the Emerging Models Project encountered everywhere, spontaneously and unscripted, is the depth of the identity of pastoral leaders as a sacramental people.

Without exception the Eucharist is understood as essential to the life of the community. Pastoral leaders were reluctant to embrace a future where this is compromised.

> *Our spiritually healthy community has its roots and nourishment in Sunday Eucharist. When nourished by the word and communion, parishioners focus on their baptismal call. (Pastoral Associate, Northeast)*

> *Our spirituality is eucharistic centered, daily adoration of the Blessed Sacrament; emphasis on good eucharistic liturgy (Mass) and sacraments. (Pastor, Southeast)*

*Our parish is one that gathers together and is nour-
ished and nurtured by the Eucharist. (Pastoral Associate,
Southwest)*

*Yes, because we have a sense of community, family, and
we have good liturgical celebrations and devotions that
help people to maintain and grow in relationship with
God and one another. (Deacon, Pacific Northwest)*

*I see in our community a living faith that is centered in
Eucharist and in common values. (Parish Life Coordinator,
Pacific Northwest)*

*I believe deanery models of parishes connected over
time and space will be tried for years until this fails. Then,
we will proceed to a people-based, need-based structure in which work will be done in outreach and Eucharist
will sustain it. (Pastor, Northeast)*

There is a longing for the table fellowship described in
Scripture. Where people experience a separation from the
eucharistic table, there is pain. Whether the separation is
caused by the nonavailability of ordained to preside or by a
felt sense of exclusion from the table, there is clarity about
the common sense of longing. Pastoral leaders express their
understanding of the parish as "an event taking place again
and again, not a society structurally instituted in a permanent way."[6]

However, even in this country, access to Eucharist is ebbing. This concern was expressed, repeatedly and unscripted.
Can we be a eucharistic people if we only have access to the

Eucharist once a month? Once a week? On a day other than Saturday or Sunday? Pastoral leaders are very clear. They do not want to lose access to the Eucharist, and they want it presided over by the ordained. While they have a sense they are being invited into a larger understanding of what it means to be a eucharistic people, their feelings are echoed in the words of theologian Patricia Fox: where "these communities . . . [are] being denied the possibility of celebrating Eucharist, [they] are also being denied the possibility of becoming the Body of Christ, of *literally* being church."[7]

The Absence of Spiritual Vitality

Whenever respondents told us their parish was not spiritually vital and alive, one or more of the following characteristics were described:

- dysfunctional pastor and/or staff
- parishioners unwilling to grow
- parish trauma

> *Liturgically, our parish is not as alive as it was in the past. Major staff changes have had an impact. From a service and outreach perspective, we are thriving and growing. We are reaching out and building relationships far beyond our church borders. A new pastoral staff person is infusing much energy into this area of parish life (hope). (Pastoral Associate, North Central)*

> *My parish is experiencing a decline because of leadership that ignores problems and cannot deal with criticism. Problems are not addressed. Parishioners have left in*

droves because the feelings of the laity have never been heard. People go elsewhere to Mass. Pastor needs some type of evaluation for anger and depression. (Diocesan Representative, North Central)

The parish has come out of an experience of scandal. (One pastor stole parish funds ten years ago.) A level of trust has been reestablished. The community is growing. The level of participation has greatly increased and contributions are strong. (Pastor, Southwest)

Our parish community is unfortunately divided into the Hispanic group and the English-speaking group. We have overflowing Mass attendance in the Spanish Masses and a full (not overflowing) attendance at English Masses. We have a strong RCIA and confirmation program. We have good chairs in both groups, but our proclaimers need more training. We are in limbo right now because our pastor is moving out and we don't know who will replace him. (Pastoral Leader, Southwest)

The pastor struggles with an addiction to alcohol. His anger and unpredictability have led to decreased participation in parish life. (Diocesan Representative, Southwest)

Two parishes—one small [with] 400 families; one larger [with] 1,700 families. The smaller one is recovering from a downward spiral and is just regaining its spirituality. The larger one is in a state of spiritual transition. This is because of population shifts and the accompanying spiritual characteristics. (Pastor, Mid-Atlantic)

The emerging operative ecclesiology of parish appears to identify parish as one of communion, inclusion, and Eucharist. These are three constitutive elements of the spirituality of parish. They are in the "bone and marrow" of the pastoral leaders in the symposia.

III
TOTAL MINISTERING COMMUNITIES

6

The Leadership Factor

The mandate of the Emerging Models Project was to study excellence in parish pastoral leadership. In developing the studies, the decision was made to focus on leadership as a system of relationships through which the community is led, rather than on the leader as a single person. This meant studying the leadership roles of the entire parish: pastor, staff, and parishioner.

When viewed through this lens, what was discovered is a blossoming of pastoral leadership roles that work together to stimulate vibrant and spiritually alive parish communities. In short, rather than finding "cookie-cutter" models of emerging parish leadership structures, the symposia identified a vibrant and creative undercurrent of parish revitalization and formation. These emerging communities are celebratory, vibrant, and welcoming communities that understand their role as total ministering communities working together—ordained, lay ecclesial ministers, and lay volunteers alike—to achieve a comprehensive vision of the parish of the future.

These communities are very often mission focused in serving the church and the world and more deeply intentional in the faith formation of individuals through small faith-based communities, deep-seated prayer, sacramental life, and a rock-bed foundation in the Eucharist as the center of all parish life and ministry. Pastoral leaders see the future of pastoral leadership as:

- collaborative, team-oriented leadership
- leading and sharing ministry in clustered parishes and small faith communities
- increased dependency on the leadership of lay ecclesial ministers, deacons, and parishioners
- ministry rooted in discipleship

There is hope for the future—it involves everyone working together. Lay and ordained leaders also understand that their leadership roles are distinct. The language they use for the roles of pastors, parish staff, and parishioners is different.

Evolving Roles of Parish Leaders

It is evident that over the past forty years there has been a distinct and pervasive shift in the roles of the pastor, staff, and parishioners. No longer is the pastor considered the sole provider of ministry and leadership in the parish.

> *The pastor is an enabler, and empowers the gifts of the people. The vision of the staff's role is to work alongside and provide resources for the lay leaders in the parish. The model of leadership they employ is a grassroots approach. The people closest to the needs . . . who are ministering to those needs are enabled and empowered to find the solutions and ways to best meet the needs. (Pastoral Associate, Mid-Atlantic)*

What is emerging is an organic whole, where the roles of pastor, staff, and parishioner are critical, interdependent, and unique. The Spirit is calling *all* the baptized to participate in providing a welcoming eucharistic community. Pastoral leaders believe the future of parish leadership is in "total ministering communities." This emerging model of leadership is rooted in the belief that the baptized have been initiated into a community of faith as disciples. They are called to care for and support one another and sent out into the world as evangelizers. The parish community discerns its vision and mission to catechize, support, and celebrate the sacraments as the mission of Jesus. Leadership is seen as "First, the ability of a person or group to articulate a vision; second, it is the ability to engage a group of people to help to make that vision a reality. Both parts are needed for good leadership."[8]

Pope Benedict XVI referred to this growing understanding of the role of the entire community in leadership when he told a group of Italian priests that the church is being called to "co-responsibility":

> I believe that this is one of the important and positive results of the Council: the co-responsibility of the entire parish, for the parish priest is no longer the only one to animate everything. Since we all form a parish together, we must all collaborate and help so that the parish priest is not left on his own, mainly as a coordinator, but truly discovers that he is a pastor who is backed up in these common tasks in which, together, the parish lives and is fulfilled.[9]

A Total Ministering Community

Participants were asked to reflect on the extent to which their parish demonstrates a total ministering approach to community development. This includes a shared sense of leadership and responsibility among pastors, staff, and pastoral council members. The ability to create a total ministering community calls for a mind-set in which pastor and pastoral leaders see the community working together as a whole to bring about the mission. Opportunities are created for leaders to work together. The pastor, staff, council, and parishioners work together for the sake of the parish community.

> Pastor, staff, and council moving toward greater collaboration and common vision; in process of developing communities and unifying spirit between/throughout all our parish organizations; pastoral council and pastor. Held a very positive half-day retreat for parish leaders for pastoral council and pastor in which areas of high energy were identified and created a follow-up session to put intentionality into creating and realizing these dreams. (Pastoral Leader, Upper Midwest)

> Structures are in place for the parish to be a total ministering community. Staff meets twice a month. PPC and commissions (Catholic education, spiritual life, human concerns, and parish life) each meet monthly. The quality of communication and collaboration could improve, as could our interaction with other parishioners. (Pastoral Associate, Upper Midwest)

It is equally part of the mind-set to be aware of the many different components of the parish and find ways to include everyone.

> To be a total ministering community, the staff, community, and pastor have to reach out to the community. Our

pastor and pastoral assistant are very good at listening to the needs of the parish and, for lack of better words, actually caring. We provide room for parishioners to take leadership roles and become active, but also try to reach those who are more introverted through spiritual endeavors—extra Masses or services, faith groups, etc. We are very involved in social justice, reaching out to the poor, sick, imprisoned, and outcast, and we try to minister to the minorities as best we can (despite language barriers), but it's equally important to our parish to have fun and develop relationships. (Pastoral Leader, Southeast)

We have broken down the geography of our parish into eight areas. Of those eight areas, we have home church leaders and bible studies that meet for those in that neighborhood. Then we have elders from each area and one elder overall who meets with the pastor. They meet once a quarter with the pastor. We have been told for ten years that we need to organize because one day soon we will not have a priest, so we've been organizing for that day. That day came on April 15 (eleven days ago). (Pastoral Leader, Southeast)

A total ministering community is a people who pray together, advise, listen together, and have a unified vision of the future. We minister to one another—white, Hispanic, people of color—and bring us together. (Pastoral Council Representative, Southeast)

The parish pastoral council plays a significant role in ministering communities and is often considered as having a constitutive role in the life and direction of the parish. Over time, parishioners understand that they also have a responsibility for the life of the parish.

> *PC members are assigned as liaisons to each of the parish ministers, so there is a communication thread back and forth. Staff meetings provide for seeing each ministry in the light of the whole, not as separate entities. (Pastoral Leader, South)*

> *The model uses the Council of Ministries in which all staff participates—not necessarily as the leaders. Pastor and lay staff meet weekly, but also monthly as part of the Council of Ministries. (Pastoral Leader, South)*

Leadership of Parishioners

In the United States today there are more than 64 million Catholics, about a third of whom are actively involved in parish life. They are increasingly young and culturally diverse. More than half are under age fifty, and half of those under the age of thirty-five are Spanish speaking. Their leadership in the parish through parish pastoral councils and other forms of parish leadership is growing. Their role as the community of disciples in carrying out the mission of the church must be the starting point and central focus, with the evolving roles of staff and pastor understood in relationship to it. This emphasis was so central to the Project findings that it is included as one of the twelve best practices for parish leaders. Parishioners stand with their pastor and staff as they serve the world together, rather than waiting to be served.

> I think we can expect a greater participation in leadership from the laity and should be preparing them and the community at large for the possibilities. Our church will survive and it will change. The greatest thing we can do is keep reminding people that change is inevitable and pray as a community that the spirit will guide the parish and inspire and call leaders. We also need to help people remember we are part of a worldwide community. As change occurs, it would be beneficial if collaboration extended beyond parish boundaries within the U.S. and draw upon the wisdom of the church leadership in other countries. (Pastoral Leader, Northeast)

As far back as the early church the assumption has been that "all believers would participate in the building up of the community and its mission to the world."[10] The concept of a fully active community, as a responsibility of baptism, is at the heart of the Vatican II documents. The revised Code of Canon Law reflects a specific understanding of the role of each of the baptized in the community where "the relationship between the individual and God . . . finds visible manifestation in the person's incorporation into Christ and the community of faith through the sacrament of baptism."[11] The Code develops this by stating that the clergy and the laity have interdependent roles in maintaining the church. Canon 208 declares that the true equality regarding the dignity and action of the Christian faithful requires the church to recognize the roles of both the laity and the clergy in its salvific mission.

The U.S. bishops stated the following in *Co-Workers in the Vineyard of the Lord*, their most recent document on parish leadership: "All the baptized are called to work toward the transformation of the world. Some do this by working in the secular realm; some do this by working in the church and focusing on the building of ecclesial communities, which has among its purposes the transformation of the world."[12] When the leadership of the parish community is focused in the discipleship of the entire community, then the parish becomes the dynamic, concrete, localized church in the world, envisioned by Vatican II.

Active parishes have many lay-led ministries, often with training and evaluation, and parishioners are developing new ministries, especially outreach. Parishes where parishioners are engaged in the growth of the parish have active and integral parish pastoral councils.

> Many provide leadership and run programs in the parish. They live and witness the gospel in the community. They work with other Catholic churches and ecumenical groups to provide outreach programs and social-justice activities. Surface and articulate the needs of the community, especially councils and boards. (Diocesan Representative, Southwest)

> The outreach to the poor has opened the door for many parishioners to step forward and assume leadership roles in organizing the various programs for feeding and giving shelter to the poor and homeless. (Pastoral Leader, Mid-Atlantic)

> Pastoral council is slowly becoming the visioning group for the parish. They spent the past year interviewing

parishioners, visioning, and setting priorities around two critical areas: building lively faith in parishioners and their active participation in mission of parish. (Diocesan Representative, Northeast)

By our model and its structure, the community provides a huge leadership role. We have an extremely large percentage of parishioners who are active in over a hundred ministries. The number of ministries demands that we have a great deal of leadership at many levels. (Diocesan Representative, South)

Pastoral leaders in today's parishes are also dealing with a growing cultural diversity, as in this parish in the Pacific Northwest:

Our pastor, staff, and council consciously work together with the use of weekly staff meetings, council meetings. Spanish pastoral leader meetings and committee/commission meetings. It is difficult and uneven with fifty-six different countries of origin. (Pastor, Southeast)

Not all parishioners are engaged, however. When speaking of parishioners that are not engaged, pastoral leaders consistently indicated a lack of empowerment, dominance by some parishioners, an expectation on the part of parishioners that the pastor must be the leader, or a lack of a significant role for the parish pastoral council.

I am not sure to what degree the community is aware that it is their role to provide leadership, since they are still indoctrinated in a Vatican I model, where the pastor does everything. (Pastor, Upper Midwest)

We have a pastoral council elected by the community. Finance council, some commissions, but little communication of plan, priorities, and budget between them all. Staff and council meetings are basically a survey of the pastor's personal calendar followed by a look at parish calendar and never issues. Staff and council never mix. Plan, pray, anything! (Pastoral Leader, Pacific Northwest)

We are working hard to build collaboration and consensus. Some still want Father to do everything, and Father struggles to find a balance between taking proper responsibility and letting go. The staff, too, is working to get more parishioners involved as volunteers. (Pastor, South)

In a separate survey for the Project conducted by the National Pastoral Life Center, pastors were asked to rate the indicators of parish vitality. Responding to a list of more than twenty marks of healthy parish life, pastors indicated that the least attention is being paid to what many pastoral leaders say is the future of the parish—namely, the formation of parishioners! On average, parishes report the lowest level of pastoral excellence in the following five areas[13]:

- the building and renewal of adult faith in all its efforts
- training of parishioners for leadership and ministry
- actively involving youth and young adults in the life of the parish
- small faith-sharing communities and/or parish-based pastoral movements

- having parishioners that are eager to become involved in parish leadership and ministry.

Increasingly, as roles evolve, parishioners will be called to minister to one another, often in small faith-based communities, and to take on responsibility for the administration of their parishes. In order to accommodate this growing reality, parishes will need to provide training and formation for lay leaders.

Leadership of Parish Staff

The Emerging Models Project chose to focus on the parish pastoral staff as a leadership cohort. This includes lay ecclesial ministers, deacons, and other laity. The makeup of parish staffs is complicated. There are recognized positions, such as pastoral associate and director of religious education, that are held by lay ecclesial ministers or deacons who are trained and qualified. There are positions that are full- or part-time, paid or not. Other positions are held by laity but not referred to as lay ecclesial ministry. And finally there are deacons who serve within the parish community as deacons on a part-time or full-time basis.

More than 31,000 lay ecclesial ministers are employed at least half-time in parish positions. Parishes also depend on other lay staff, such as business managers, teachers, and, increasingly, deacons. The U.S. bishops spent ten years studying the role and place of the laity in church service and ministry, publishing in 2005 their document, *Co-Workers in the Vineyard of the Lord.* Here they acknowledge lay ecclesial ministry as a growing reality, rooted in the sacraments of initiation and having a place within the community of the church, whose communion and mission it serves.[14] The work of lay ecclesial ministry is inextricably bound to the community that it serves and cannot exist outside that community, just as pastoring exists in and for the sake of the community.

The ministry and formation of deacons is described in the *National Directory for the Formation, Ministry, and Life of Permanent Deacons in the United States*, which was published in 2004. Grounded in an ecclesiology of *communio*, the *Directory* spells out the role of the deacon in the parish.[15] However, unlike the lay ecclesial minister, the deacon is ordained for service to the diocesan church (*Directory*, 257) and "exercises his ministry within a specific pastoral context—the communion and mission of a diocesan church (*Directory*, 41)."[16]

There are 16,000 deacons in this country, a growing and formed cohort of pastoral leaders. They embody the very heart of parish life, of *communio et missio*, or going beyond the parish to care for the poor. The permanent diaconate reminds us of our absolute call to preach the Good News to the poor, and then to return to animate the community for service. More dioceses have deacon-formation programs, but it is clear that, despite the documents on the permanent diaconate, there is no real consensus on the role of deacons *in the parish*, or on the work and witness they provide.

Parishes depend on other lay staff as well—business managers, principals, teachers, and others. The parish of the future, according to the Project participants, will have an increased dependency on lay-led communities in general, and on the leadership of lay ecclesial ministers, deacons, and parishioners in particular.

What became evident throughout the Emerging Models Project was that the parish staff plays a significant role in serving the life of the community. As participants spoke of the leadership of those on staff, it became apparent that this group was providing much of the day-to-day ministry and presence at the parish. Parish staff tend to the pastoral (though not sacramental) care of the community, coordinate parish programming, and focus on and call forth the gifts of the individual members of the community. They may be the sole pastoral presence at any given moment, meeting the needs of parishioners, often serving as generalists where once they were able to serve as specialists focused on a specific area of parish ministry.

> The staff provides well-educated individuals in special-ized ministries (liturgy/music, pastoral care, religious edu-cation/youth ministry, etc.) to serve and empower the community in implementing the mission and respond to the needs of the parish. (Pastor, Southeast)

> The staff serves as guides, mentors, support, liaisons, again empowering others to take the ball and run, knowing that others are there for encouragement and support. Often the staff are the ones who provide the personal invitation to parishioners to become leaders. (Pastoral Leader, South)

> The leadership role of our staff is primarily now one of empowerment and enablement of others as volunteers or employees in the educational, social, and pastoral ministries of our parish, specifically by providing education, forma-tion, training, and support for ministry, as well as recruitment and screening in many areas. (Pastor, North Central)

Expertise in particular areas; recruiting, training, and support of parishioner leaders. The two pastoral associates and pastoral minister each take responsibility for one or more ministry areas across the entire parish, as well as provide on-site presence at two worship sites each. (Diocesan Representative, Northeast)

Both lay and ordained leaders agreed on what the leadership of staff entails. Where done well, there is a collaborative team atmosphere and strong leadership roles.

The model for the parish is collaborative. No one acts in isolation. All ministry in the parish is to happen through the coordinated efforts of teams/staff with the laity. (Pastor, Mid-Atlantic)

Most staff direction is aimed toward the various children's and youth programs. After five years experience (which isn't much, I agree), I believe that more staff allows for more collaboration and empowerment of people; the more, the better (provided they are truly collaborative and are able to keep the bigger vision in mind). Right now, I believe our staff is maxed out—we'd like more, but money is scarce. It is a frustrating place to be. (Pastor, Northeast)

Where staff leadership is hindered, pastoral leaders speak of weak team dynamics, a controlling leadership style on the part of the pastor or parish life coordinator, or a lack of resources.

Staff members like me are allowed limited leadership appropriate to their position, such as time management and deciding how to implement decisions made by the pastor. It didn't always used to be like this and I am having difficulty sometimes with this adjustment. (Pastoral Leader, North Central)

The pastor is in charge. A few lay leaders were hired out of necessity. The associate priest is following the letter of the law. Deacons are unsure of their role. Lay leaders are discouraged by the lack of true collaboration. (Diocesan Representative, Mid-Atlantic)

Leadership Role of Pastors

In a country that had become used to having many clergy serving in parishes, the emerging demographics are sobering. The number of clergy available for pastoring parishes is diminishing far faster than it is being replenished. The majority of U.S. dioceses have more parishes than they have pastors, and nearly half of all parishes share their pastor with at least one other parish or mission.[17] As priest-pastors take on the responsibility of megaparishes or multiple parishes in addition to sacramental ministry in other parishes, their role is evolving. When lay and ordained leaders speak of the role of pastor they use a very specific language that is both theological and practical.

Participants spoke of pastors as facilitators, presiding over the life of the community as well as over sacramental life. Whether facilitating the life of the parish, the staff, the council, or the vision, this role is evident in the responses of both lay and ordained pastoral leaders. Pastors call forth the gifts of the community and are the gatekeepers of change. They hold the broader vision of the parish, a sense of its mission, and guide the community where it needs to move. Lay and ordained pastoral leaders are recognizing that the role of the pastor is evolving, honoring the unique and needed gift they bring to parish life.

> *Pastor sets a vision for the parish. He works in collaboration with the staff. He recognizes and affirms the gifts in the parish. He calls forth gifts and leadership from the parish. (Pastor, North Central)*

> *Facilitator and vision director for those who are committed to leadership and involvement. (Deacon, South)*

> *Our pastor is the convener of the staff and various parish groups. He is the person who calls the community back to its vision and mission. (Pastoral Associate, Southwest)*

> *Builds relationships with the community and helps them build relationships with each other. Responsible to create a culture of relationships. Looks for and builds new leaders. Encourages the use of various gifts in the community. (Parish Life Coordinator, Mid-Atlantic)*

It is important to note that, as the role of the pastor evolves in the contemporary church, it continues to be deeply rooted in the earliest understandings of the church, recalling the role of leader in the Pauline letters as the one to whom oversight of the community has been given.

When described in relational terms, the role of the one pastoring can also be applied to parish life coordinators, or those providing leadership under Canon 517.2. The difference is that their leadership of the community, while providing oversight, does not include presiding over the sacramental life of the community, even though they provide for essential dimensions of that sacramental life in planning and teaching.

Parish Life Coordinators (Canon 517.2)

The Emerging Models Project conducted the first extensive study of the use of Canon 517.2—the installation by the bishop of deacons, religious, or laypeople to provide the pastoral and administrative leadership of a parish where there is no resident pastor. This canon has been in use for over twenty years in this country.

The 1983 revised *Code of Canon Law* affirms this calling in various ministerial areas, including the "care of souls" that takes place within a parish. This is an activity centered on the church's responsibility to teach, sanctify, and govern the people of God. "Full care of souls" is entrusted to priests (Canon 150) but partial care is a responsibility that can be shared by many, including laity, deacons, and vowed religious. It is this collaborative model and the baptismal call to service that form the basis for understanding Canon 517.2.[18]

Originally, parish life coordinators (one of over thirty titles for this position) were women religious. Today the majority continue to be women religious, with another 25 percent being deacons, and 25 percent being laypersons. Under this canon, sacramental ministry is provided by priests who are either appointed by the bishop or recruited by the PLC. Some parish life coordinators have a list of over fifty priests they call on a rotating basis to provide sacramental ministry. Some begin calling priests in the fall to ensure there is a presider for the Triduum!

The work of the parish life coordinator is to oversee the activities of individuals and groups who serve as staff and parish leaders, and to provide pastoral care on a daily basis to the people of the parish. In doing so, she or he is supervised by a priest moderator and collaborates with one or more priests who serve as sacramental ministers. This may be the major share of the leadership of the parish in all but the sacramental roles reserved to priests.[19]

Where the bishop formally installs a PLC, there is a positive impact in all aspects of the ministry over time. PLCs love their ministry, like many pastors, preferring the pastoral work to the administrative work. Collaboration between the sacramental minister and the PLC, working together to help the community understand its role, is key to the success of this model.

Pastoral Leadership Models

Participants were asked to describe their model of leadership. Where there was an intentional model, three primary styles surfaced. These models of active leadership are 1) collaborative, empowering the baptismal call of the community; 2) centered on a core staff; or 3) the traditional pastor-centered model. Each of the models has a different focus or starting point. Each is dependent on the preference of the pastor, and all are partially driven by resources, demographics, or parishioner vision.

Intentionally collaborative/shared ministry

Many pastoral leaders described their leadership model as one that is collaborative, with shared ministry of the baptized.

Supported by pastor and staff, this model is focused on calling forth and engaging the gifts of the community. Participation of the laity is key to this model. Their engagement in the mission of the parish is seen as the goal of this leadership model in which leadership is provided by councils, committees, and commissions, with the staff playing a significant supportive role. To provide for the needs and concerns of the parish the community engages in visioning, formation, consultation, consensus building, and goal setting. Parishioners work together, assuming responsibility for their community. This model is concerned with assuring the role of women in parish leadership.

Predominant in the South and Southeast, this model is also the most used in connection with PLC-led communities where dependence on the hierarchy is not an option. Pastors and staff using this model are more likely to speak of servant leadership, seeing themselves as animators. They describe themselves as open and committed to mutual relationships with parishioners as they work together to build the community and service beyond the community. They understand that parishioners have a greater responsibility for the life of the community than was understood in the past and work to develop their gifts for moving the community forward.

> *Pastor and school principal believe in delegation of authority and responsibility. All pastoral staff members model good leadership skills. Councils, committees, and organizations are effective in fulfilling functions and responsibilities. Individual parishioners take initiative for parish events, etc. (Pastor, South)*

Ministries are divided into five areas of parish life. Ministerial leaders come together to look at issues, needs, and find solutions. We use the consensus model and work toward a solution until all can buy in—yielding no winners or losers. Two reps from each core community make up the pastoral council—PC is where everything is coordinated, communicated. The other parish follows a similar model in that the people who are involved in ministry, those who are closest to the people, know the real needs and come together as pastoral committees for worship, faith formation, Hispanic-ministry oversight, temporal administration, patrimony, and stewardship. (Pastoral Associate, Mid-Atlantic)

We are intentional on being an empowering community that calls forth the gifts of the parish members. The parish is incorporating a covenant model. For several years, we have worked on a model of a parish with only a part-time pastor needing leadership from within the community. The recent pastor promoted this as he drew near to retirement. (Pastoral Associate, Northeast)

We have one pastor, five priests who are helping, thirty-five staff who are full- and part-time. Eighty-six people are on the pastoral council. Forty-eight people are on the finance council. There are a total of 175 people who work together in this level of leadership, but there are more members on commissions and organizations and committees. (Pastor, Pacific Northwest)

*We are in the process of building a pastoral leader-
ship team based on the presumption that "leadership"
is a charism and ministry of the church not limited to the
ordained and characterized by collaboration, accountability, mutual responsibility and support, and effective
communication. We are also in the process of establishing the lay advisory councils with the right and responsibility of participating in all decisions that affect the life,
welfare, and ministry of our parish: pastoral council,
school board, and stewardship and development councils. (Pastor, North Central)*

Centered on a core team

Many pastoral leaders describe their parish leadership model
as centered on a core team, placing staff and personnel at the
center of their leadership model. Knowing who is ensuring
the life of the parish is important. This model is described as
corporate, with the pastor, or parish life coordinator, and staff
coordinating the ministry of the parish and ensuring its sacramental life. A significant role for the parish council exists as
an advisory board to those who conduct the day-to-day work
of the parish. The support of parishioners is elicited. However,
the primary focus appears to be on providing the sacramental,
pastoral, and catechetical life of the parish.

*Priest/pastor with pastoral associate/deacon and reli-
gious order priest. We have a pastoral team including
business manager, youth minister, liturgical director, principal, and DRE. Priest/pastor uses collaborative pastoral*

team concept to meet needs of the parish. We have a ministry council and are forming a pastoral council and finance council. (Deacon, Southwest)

Our leadership is pretty much the pastor and the other priests (parochial vicar and priest in residence). We have a limited staff for a parish of 1,500 families. The school principal is the most active lay ecclesial minister. (Diocesan Representative, Southwest)

Pastor who works with sizeable staff: newly ordained priests, extern (all three priests share in providing sacramental ministry to all six worship sites), two pastoral associates, one pastoral minister, director of faith formation, director of sacramental preparation, and business manager. (Diocesan Representative, Northeast)

Centered around the pastor

The third model described by pastoral leaders is the traditional pastor-centered model. The pastor in this model has a strong sense of being responsible for the parish and ensuring parish life. These pastors are described as having a strong sense of needing to run the parish, to be in charge, sometimes to the point of micromanaging, in order to ensure that the life of the community is provided for. While all models are dependent on the decision of the pastor, this model most reflects the pastor's need to ensure parish life. It is more likely than other models to be used where there is part-time staff or limited resources. It may be used in parishes where parishioners continue to believe that everything should be done by the pastor.

Ministry is developed through meetings and the accomplishment of tasks and depends on the goodwill of parishioners to participate in the work of the parish. In this model, little mention is made of the role of parish staff.

> In my Hispanic community, the leadership model expected is a top-down clerical model where the priest makes all the decisions. (Pastoral Leader, South)

> Current pastor for eighteen years brought lone-ranger style that prevented cooperation and collaboration. Over time, lay leaders had to give up and let go of any effort to be effective collaborators. (Pastoral Leader, South)

> The pastor and priests are at the helm inviting staff and parishioners to assist them. (Pastoral Leader, Mid-Atlantic)

In the end, a faith community that is being sustained and nourished, where the dignity and sacredness of individuals are affirmed and respected, is the most significant sign of the presence of good pastoral leadership. In the presence of good and faithful pastoral ministry, there is ongoing growth and development within the community, and attention is paid to the personal and spiritual development of individuals. The community is called to experience a clear prophetic challenge rooted in the Gospel, and is called to build up the reign of God.

Changes in leadership and parish structures are happening throughout the United States. Those involved often expressed the belief that these changes were solely local. However, they are not. As pastoral leaders speak with one another, new ideas and an understanding of the scope of change are becoming apparent. The emerging models of leadership and parish structures call for a new worldview, one that allows us to see the invitation and gift of the Spirit as it emerges. This change is organic, happening throughout the structure, moving forward as the Spirit invites. It is now the task of the church to begin understanding the theological implications of these changes and how they are consistent with the tradition of the church.

7

Marks of Excellence:
Personal and Professional

The Project studied marks of excellence in pastoral leadership. The characteristics of being ethical, pastoral, prophetic, collaborative, inclusive, and welcoming bear special relevance to the spiritual life of the parish. While there are many ways to be a leader, the spirituality of a parish calls for those behaviors that call forth the ability of parishioners to bring about the kingdom in their lives, in the parish, and in the world. As pastoral leaders discussed their understanding of these qualities, their practice fell into two categories: personal qualities and professional practices. Listed below are the marks of excellence along with their definitions, which were provided to participants at the beginning of the symposia.

ETHICAL: Appropriate Behavior in Service to the Community

Ethical leaders respect the dignity of the person. They are faithful to the Gospel and the mission and ministry of Jesus. They exhibit appropriate behavior in both the personal and professional arenas.

Personal and professional standards of ethical leaders do affect the parish. The integrity of pastoral leaders and the congruence of their beliefs, practices, and actions impact the community and its spirituality. Catholic leaders have come a long way in understanding the need for this mark, especially in the wake of the abuse crisis. Commenting on ethical behaviors, leaders focus both on professional praxis and personal integrity, along with a respect for the boundaries of others. They call for transparency in organizational standards. They believe that in the future a greater sense of accountability, ethics, and integrity will be the marks of ethical leadership.

The ethical qualities most frequently mentioned are organizational practices that respect the dignity of others. These practices include professionalism, observing confidentiality, and holding good boundaries. In personal ethics, leaders need to exhibit authenticity, integrity, and honesty.

- Personal Qualities
  » integrity
  » honesty
  » personal ethics
  » accountability
  » authenticity
  » openness
  » trustworthiness
- Professional Praxis
  » professionalism
  » offering respect, dignity, and confidentiality
  » honoring boundaries
  » inclusive, fair, and equitable
  » respect for the dignity and confidentiality of others
  » just organizational and financial practices, employment practices, systems of checks and balances, and transparency

PASTORAL: Serving the Shared Life of the Community

Pastoral leaders are called to be faithful to the mission of the church and to the building up of the kingdom. They must be able to care for the overall welfare and needs of the community, while empowering the members of the community to care for one another.

The call to be pastoral is foundational and informs each of the marks of excellence. It is an intrinsic way of being. When leaders speak of being pastoral they most frequently mention a strong relational presence with people and a commitment to shared responsibility and empowerment. They include collaboration as well as support for the needs of the parish community. Being servant leaders means holding gospel-centered leadership and value as important priorities.

Professionally, pastoral leaders serve the needs of the community with a clear vision and direction for pastoral care and support. Pastoral activities are based on accountability and transparency. Pastoral leaders focus on developing skills for being pastoral, including the ability to be relational and provide a listening presence. While setting clear ministerial boundaries they learn to be compassionate, including the disenfranchised in their care.

- Personal Qualities
  - » good listener
  - » strong relational presence
  - » compassionate
  - » passion, sensitivity, and awareness
  - » clear ministerial boundaries

- Professional Praxis
  - » understanding and serving the needs of the community
  - » shared responsibility and empowerment
  - » engaging the gifts of the community in service to one another
  - » facilitating outreach to the disenfranchised

PROPHETIC: Speaking and Witnessing to the Word of God

Prophetic leaders move the parish in a direction that is faithful to the Gospel and into mission. They are ecumenical, evangelistic, justice focused, and mission directed, providing outreach to the community. They are servant leaders, concerned about being faithful to the ministry of the church while at the same time building the kingdom.

Communities need prophetic leaders who root the life of the community in the Gospel and invite the community to hear and respond to God's invitation. Participants thought that this is the most difficult of the marks to put into practice. Being prophetic includes a faithful and prophetic stance toward justice, a commitment to share vision, and fidelity to the Gospels. These participants believe that understanding the environment and building a shared commitment among parishioners is essential to their prophetic role.

Prophetic leaders exhibit a faithful and prophetic stance toward justice, committed to holding and modeling a shared vision of justice as an important priority. In fact, it appears that having a sense of social justice is intrinsic to the self-identity of pastoral leaders. Prophetic leaders speak of offering a faithful witness to a sense of justice inside the church and in the world, and strongly believe this stance must involve a commitment to being rooted in the biblical tradition.

Professionally, prophetic leaders recognize they must be willing to make unpopular decisions and speak difficult truths to and for the community. Being prophetic often calls leaders into ecumenical and interreligious dialogue. In order to lead a faith community in this way, the prophetic leader must be a person of prayer, rooted in Scripture, willing to provide personal witness to justice in the church and in the world.

- Personal Qualities
  - » person of prayer, rooted in Scripture
  - » personal witness to justice in the church and in the world
  - » offers hope and vision
  - » calls for courage
- Professional Praxis
  - » speaks to and for the community
  - » justice and fidelity to the Gospel, rooted in prayer and spirituality
  - » addresses difficult issues truthfully
  - » Forms a prophetic awareness in others

COLLABORATIVE: Engaging the Gifts of the Community

Collaborative leaders engage the gifts of all the baptized, working together toward a shared mission. They bring the fullness of the Catholic tradition to the community: communal, sacramental, pastoral, and prophetic. They respect the Spirit that is present and active in the community and in its members.

A common understanding of collaboration is that it describes a way for people to work together. Pastoral leaders often find it challenging to coordinate collaborative efforts among male-female teams and among ordained and nonordained professional staff. Identifying and nurturing best practices for collaboration is a critically important task.

Collaboration also means calling forth the best in others. This means recognizing the baptismal call of parishioners and calling forth the gifts of the community. Collaborative pastoral leaders delegate and facilitate opportunities for others to share gifts. They recognize a mutual accountability in a faith community and a commitment to shared decision making and planning. They understand the role of subsidiarity in the parish community, and have a strong commitment to shared prayer and discernment.

While collaborative leaders have come to understand and believe in the baptismal call of all the faithful, there is less understanding of how to actually empower this call. Pastoral leaders often focus on the activity of the community within the parish and do not reflect on the need to empower the baptized to carry their faith into the world. These collaborative skills are of great interest to pastoral leaders but the least well developed in their experience.

- Personal Qualities
  - » offering discernment and respect
  - » listening to the needs of the community
  - » learning to work together

- Professional Praxis
  - » focused on engaging the community
  - » committed to shared decision making and planning
  - » developing a shared vision for the community
  - » calling forth the gifts and wisdom of the community to serve a shared vision
  - » creating opportunities for shared prayer and discernment

INCLUSIVE and WELCOMING: Creating a Sense of Belonging

Welcoming leaders ensure that all who desire a closer relationship to God are genuinely received and welcomed in a spirit of heartfelt hospitality, openness, and eagerness both to give and to receive. They invite, support, and animate diversity in the parish, paying particular attention to diverse cultures, languages, ethnicities, genders, generations, abilities, and beliefs—in ways that are respectful and mutually enriching.

Inclusive and welcoming leaders have an intentional ministry of welcoming and hospitality. Welcoming leaders order inclusive behaviors into two distinct categories. First, they call for a strong multicultural awareness as the demographics of U.S. parishes change. The reality of parish life is that it is multicultural and diverse. Pastoral leaders are required to celebrate the Eucharist and minister in multiple languages. Increasingly, too, intergenerational diversity is becoming a challenge as younger generations interact with church differently from their parents and grandparents. Young adults are bringing new questions and longing for a deeper understanding of the liturgy.

Second, they speak of taking an active role in calling forth the gifts and leadership of all parishioners, including diverse people, cultures, lifestyles, and life circumstances in parish life. They are learning how to recognize and call forth leadership within diversity. They see their role as one of building awareness and acceptance of diversity within the community, even when that community is a linked, clustered, or mega parish.

On an individual level, they describe the need to develop their own personal awareness and abilities. It would be advantageous to be bilingual. Professionally, there is a need for diversity training and sensitivity, so that they can lead the community in creating open, accessible, hospitable communities. They name this as the mark of excellence they are least successful in accomplishing. Yet if this is a hallmark of the spirituality of a parish and our tradition, then attention needs to be given to how leaders are recognizing the "stranger in our midst."

- Personal Qualities
  - » welcoming
  - » aware of, and curious about, differences
  - » multilingual and multiculturally aware
  - » teaching by example, personal effort
- Professional Praxis
  - » creating inclusive, open, and inviting communities
  - » multicultural awareness and sensitivity
  - » aware of different gifts, needs
  - » inviting and hospitable

» including diverse people, cultures, and life circumstances in parish life
» engaging a diversity of parish members
» creating an accessible and welcoming environment

What came as a surprise was that excellent pastoral leaders often demonstrate two additional qualities: *creativity* and *adaptivity*. Pastoral leaders are creative. They seem to have a "pastoral imagination" that enables them to make traditional practices available and accessible in their communities. They find new ways to work with what they have and make it new. Pastoral leaders are also adaptive. Adaptive leaders are those who find themselves in situations where there is no precedent, no experience, and conventional wisdom does not work. These leaders are willing to roll up their sleeves, sit with the community to find new answers, and work collaboratively to create what is needed. They recognize that the changing circumstances in which they find themselves call for new ways of thinking, new answers, new skills, and the engagement of the community in finding solutions. They seem to be able to engage people in facing the challenge, changing perspectives, and working through differences and conflict while holding the faith and vision of the community.

All pastoral leaders are challenged by the call to pastoral excellence. It appears that leaders are more able to be pastoral than collaborative, that it is easier to be welcoming than prophetic. In the end, the most significant sign of the presence of good pastoral leadership is a faith community that is being sustained and nourished, where the dignity and sacredness of individuals are affirmed and respected. In the presence of good and faithful pastoral ministry, there is ongoing growth and development within the community, and attention is paid to the personal and spiritual development of individuals. The community is called to experience the clear prophetic challenge rooted in the Gospel, to build up the reign of God. These are the marks of excellence.

IV

EMERGING
PRACTICES

8

Best Practices for Parish Excellence

The field of organizational development has utilized a concept called "benchmarking" to describe the leading-edge practices that high-performing organizations use to achieve their missions. Admittedly, the concept of "best practices" is difficult to define. In simple terms, it describes what highly functioning organizations concretely do to achieve their excellence and leadership position. Another way to think of best practices is perhaps "first principles." In other words, what are those behavioral expressions or practices that organizations and their leaders use as the first principles in determining what is essential to move forward into the future? These best practices may not necessarily be new or novel; they may be very traditional. Their key attribute is contributing to the mission success of parishes.

A number of best practices or first principles were apparent in the table conversations, large group discussions, and written responses of pastoral leaders to the twenty-seven questions they considered over the three-day symposia process. The 529 pastoral leaders who participated in these symposia may not reflect a typical or normative picture of parish leaders of the church in the United States. They were chosen by their dioceses because of the diverse roles they play in parish life. They were also chosen for their leadership contribution to parish development as "thought leaders" within their individual dioceses. These leaders were, in fact, an interesting cross section of local thought leaders who are perhaps foreshadowing the ways in which successful parishes will navigate the difficult waters of organizational change and the restructuring of parish life. These thought leaders may represent a well-grounded cohort group to determine some leading-edge "best practices" for the future of parish vitality and parish excellence.

Among the 529 symposia participants, the twelve characteristics listed below were evident in their conversations and their leadership practices. They are documented here as potential benchmarks for parish excellence, in some cases foreshadowing needed changes in parish life to sustain parish vitality.

Sacramentality of Parish Life as a Eucharistic Community

It was clear that pastoral leaders both maintain and promote a deep-seated spiritual vitality in their parishes and communities linked to the centrality of the sacraments, particularly the celebration of the Eucharist. These pastoral leaders place a high premium on the identity of their local communities as rooted in the Eucharist and the sacraments as the fundamental and defining characteristics of Catholicity in their parishes. What often troubles these pastoral leaders the most about future changes is the very real and imminent diminished access to the celebration of the Eucharist for their parishioners.

These pastoral leaders devote significant time and parish resources to the quality of celebration and catechesis which surrounds their sacramental and worship life as a parish. These pastoral leaders also give voice to significant concern that a future reliance on communion services in lieu of a full celebration of the Eucharist may contribute to a diminished Catholic identity as a parish. In a few instances, there is anecdotal evidence that parishioners without a regular celebration of the Eucharist tend to define their weekly communion services as Eucharist celebrations or "Mass" despite catechesis and diocesan guidelines to the contrary.

These pastoral leaders affirm and validate a deep connection between the spiritual vitality of their parish communities and the centrality of the celebration of the Eucharist as a "first principle." These pastoral leaders also vigorously advocate that full and regular participation in the celebration of the Eucharist by a local parish is a transformative sacramental experience and mystery not easily replaced by the availability of "holy communion." A direct link between the sacramentality and spirituality of parish life, particularly the celebration of the Eucharist, is the hallmark of these pastoral leaders and their parish experiences of excellence and transformation. These leaders place primary importance on the richness of the church's sacramental life, centered on the Eucharist. They may also emphasize in practice the quality of the catechesis and liturgy which express this tradition.

Total Ministering Community

Throughout the symposia, pastoral leaders referenced a strong commitment to the development of a "total ministering community" within their parishes. This notion of a "total ministering community" is based on a foundational call and recognition of all baptized people to discipleship. Their experience of a "total ministering community" demonstrates practical ways in which these pastoral leaders engage clergy, religious, nonordained professionals, and lay leaders in their parishes, working together to build their spiritual vitality and to express their discipleship in the world.

Pastoral leaders with a comprehensive commitment to a "total ministering community" have adapted their parish structures to engage lay leaders in a full evaluation of, and responsibility for, the future vitality of the parish and its ministries. Pastoral councils are often the focal point of pastoral planning and visioning. Formal processes are often in place for training and developing the practical skills, as well as for the spiritual formation of lay leaders as "coworkers in the vineyard" for the future development and leadership of the parish.

These pastoral leaders experience parish vitality as an undeniable consequence of a spirit of collaboration and cooperation. For these pastoral leaders, work with the laity is not so much a matter of necessity, but a matter of acknowledgement and moving forward a common baptismal call to discipleship beyond the parish as well as ministry within the parish.

Formation of Lay Ministers

Parishes and their leaders who express a deep commitment to a total ministering community have established and structured processes for the formation of lay ministers. These formation processes range from those that are organized at the parish level with a degree of informality to a comprehensive diocesan process for the formation and credentialing of lay ministers. In rural areas, these lay ministry formation processes may also be done in conjunction with local Catholic universities, special institutes, or through an online training and forma-tional experience.

The common elements in these formation processes include a structured, ongoing, and high level of engagement with groups of parishioners, usually on an annual basis, in a process of discerning their call and their fulfillment of their baptismal ministry. For some leaders, it is somewhat troubling that as dioceses and parishes experience diminishing resources, this most vital element of formation for lay ministry is often sus-pended or eliminated for financial reasons. Formal formation programs, spiritual direction, support groups, and degree-level course work are often the needed preparation for nurturing the call and establishing a foundational core of lay leaders com-mitted as "coworkers in the vineyard," sharing responsibility for building the future spiritual vitality of their parishes.

A tangible and formal commitment to the formation of these prospective lay leaders is a recurring theme or first principle which may be described as a best practice for parish excellence. Parishes are very innovative in their various forms of establishing and sustaining such lay ministry formation programs. However, these pastoral leaders appear to validate the formation of lay ministers as a needed prerequisite for communities that are demonstrating a sense of discipleship in the world.

Pastor or Parish Life Coordinator as Facilitator and Agent of Change

One of the surprising findings of the regional symposia is the role that pastors and parish life coordinators play in calling forth the gifts of leadership from among their parishioners. It may have been expected that with an increased involvement of the laity and lay leaders in parish life, the role of pastor is more clearly defined or narrowly focused as sacramental and liturgical leader. Among symposia thought leaders, this does not appear to be the case.

Without diminishing this essential role of pastors as the sacramental leaders of the parish, pastors and parish life coordinators most often report that they find themselves increasingly acting as facilitators, catalysts, and chief collaborators calling forth the gifts of others. This role often places them as change agents, calling forth new roles, new structures, and new programs to sustain the vitality of parish life. Once again, this "on-the-ground" experience of pastors and parish life coordinators points out an area in their training and formation which may not be adequately reflected in the curriculum of their seminary programs and ministry or theological degrees.

Pastors and parish life coordinators often find themselves fully engaged in leading the visioning processes of parishes, training pastoral councils in their roles and responsibilities, and facilitating the development of new projects and priorities to give birth to the future of their parishes. These pastoral leaders are often called upon to create new structures, restructure commissions and committees, and design organizational strategies that contribute to the vitality of their growing communities. This role of pastor or parish life coordinator as facilitator and change agent may reflect an understated, but critically important, reality of the skill sets and needed organizational abilities that build parish communities. These skills and roles may become even more central to leadership's ability to sustain parishes in a complex culture.

In futuring exercises during the symposia, parish leaders were asked to identify their future expectations for the roles of pastor or parish life coordinator. In their responses they often identified this emerging challenge of leading change and facilitating the gifts of others as a most significant priority for their leadership.

Pastoral Staff as Leadership Teams that Enable Ministry

Similar to the emerging roles of pastors and parish life coordinators, parish staff roles may be evolving beyond their specific theological and pastoral areas of training and education. Rather than viewing pastoral staff as individual experts who deliver or provide ministry to parishioners, symposia participants often described pastoral staff as collaborative leadership teams that facilitate and oversee the formation of lay leaders rather than administer their own projects and priorities. This emerging role of pastoral staff often includes calling forth and mentoring the gifts of others beyond the day-to-day direct ministry they provide to members of the parish.

This presents a very challenging role for future pastoral staff to balance with their core content expertise. For example, a youth minister who may have been primarily recruited to minister directly to the youth of the parish, might find himself or herself in the role of developing a team of peer ministers and adult ministers who contribute significantly to all or part of the youth ministry program. In this role, he or she functions as trainer, coordinator, planner, evaluator, and mentor. This role of pastoral staff as an enabler of the ministry and gifts of others requires skills in planning, team building, group process, program design, and program evaluation.

A wide variety of parish staff roles and experiences were represented among pastoral leaders who attended the regional symposia. However, among those who experienced significant success in the motivation and animation of lay members of their parishes, the experience of the pastoral staff has grown to encompass their new roles as enablers of the gifts and ministries of others.

The Emergent Multiculturalism as Grace

Pastoral leaders from predominantly Hispanic, Asian, or African-American parish communities were underrepresented despite efforts to identify their presence as a priority. However, many of the pastoral leaders who were present demonstrated a significant effort to embrace multiculturalism as a gift and an asset for their parishes. They experience diversity as a grace. Pastoral leaders with these multicultural experiences frequently reported that difficulties and challenges of integrating multicultural parish communities are often outweighed by the enormous benefit of multiculturalism, which brings their parishes to a new sense of identity and vitality and is therefore a grace to be celebrated.

Some pastoral leaders in the regional symposia have begun to adapt their pastoral practices. In some areas, leaders have introduced bilingual worship services in anticipation of growing diversity in their area. They are educating their parish communities on the eventual multicultural identity of the domestic church. Rather than adopting ethnocentric approaches to the future of parish ministry, these pastoral leaders have found ways to adapt and embrace the diversity of their current realities. In some instances, different leadership groups represent the needs of their "second-culture members" within parish structures. In other cases, the pastoral staff has been intentionally recruited with the language and skill sets to reach out and embrace people of different cultural and ethnic heritages. In some instances, parishes work together in an urban area for a combined ministry outreach. Special worship services and feast days, such as Our Lady of Guadalupe, have become an integral part of overall parish life. In some parishes, celebrations related to ethnic cultures and ethnic foods have become part of parish programming, fostering openness while welcoming people from diverse backgrounds and cultures. In all these experiences, multiculturalism has been embraced as a gift and a grace to the future vitality of the parish rather than as a problem to be addressed or solved.

Lifelong Catechesis

The formation of people of all ages in the life of the church appears to be a high priority for those leading-edge pastoral leaders who participated in the symposia. Many models, programs, and expressions of lifelong catechesis were evident throughout the symposia process. Some pastoral leaders have adopted a "whole community catechesis" process with a formal intergenerational faith formation program replacing former age-based approaches. Others describe a more eclectic approach to ongoing and intergenerational faith formation, citing many forms throughout parish life. These include the RCIA, RCIA "refresher programs," biblical studies courses, retreats, renewals, missions, online courses, sacramental preparation, early childhood through youth catechesis, adult formation programs, lay movements, and small faith communities.

Beneath these efforts is a shared commitment to establishing lifelong catechesis as a constituent part of the Catholic identity of their parish members. These leaders reaffirm a long-standing tradition of formation in spiritual maturity as part of the expectation for parish members.

Pastoral leaders in the symposia appear to transcend an episodic approach or the implementation of random programs for faith formation and focus instead on a more integrated and long-term approach, encouraging parishioners to see their ongoing formation in faith and the life of the church as a constitutive element of their identity and spiritual maturity. In many instances, these pastoral leaders have formal structures—including committees, boards, or commissions—providing guidance and oversight to the faith formation of the entire parish community. While the notion of lifelong faith formation is certainly not new to parish catechesis, these pastoral leaders reinforce its primary contribution to parish vitality as a "first principle" or best practice.

Intentional and Proactive Outreach to Individuals and Households

One characteristic of megachurches in the Protestant evangelical community is their ability to reach out to individuals and households through a complex network of relationships and community-involvement groups. This is a highly relational and deeply personal approach to engaging their members in the life of the community at the individual and family levels.

Among pastoral leaders who participated in the symposia, this proactive outreach to individuals and households is evident regardless of the size, diversity, and complexity of their parish structures. These pastoral leaders have found ways to reach out and invite every household to participate in the life of the parish with an invitation to learn, share, contribute, and celebrate in the future formation and development of the parish. Rather than relying on newsletters, bulletins, and announcements, they have developed a network that initiates contact with every household. In the larger parish communities, parish boards or commissions are responsible for this outreach. Special interest e-mail circulation lists, Internet blogs, and small group gatherings are more the norm than the exception.

Some parishes function only to serve those present at Sunday worship. This often leaves a significant percentage of the population within the parish untouched. Admittedly, this may create a bit of a "chicken or egg" circumstance, where one may ask if weekly participation in worship is the driver for parish participation or if an ongoing relationship with the parish promotes and encourages weekly participation in the sacramental life of the church. Perhaps both are the case.

The basic gospel principle of "knowing each by name" was highly evident among those pastoral leaders who described their communities as vibrant and welcoming. In one very poor urban community, a single parish life coordinator systematically schedules annual visits with every household. This ability to reach out to individuals with an invitation for greater participation in the parish community is a hallmark or best practice of parish excellence.

The biblical imperative that "I know mine and mine know me" is more than a scriptural passage for those who seek to build active and vibrant faith communities. It encapsulates the idea that individual and personal relationships bring people to experience their parish as community and as a significant anchoring institution for their faith lives and their service to the world.

Regional Ministry to Youth and Young Adults

Pastoral leaders employed many proactive efforts to reach youth and young adults, especially regionally or across parochial ministries. In these parish communities, leaders have structured intentional efforts to reach youth and young adults in the communities in which they live and work. They recognize that youth and young adults may not be fully engaged in the traditional forms and structures of parish ministry. Consequently, they make special efforts to reach young adult leaders and youth. In these extra-parochial settings they provide catechetical and formational programs that are age-appropriate for young adults in their twenties and thirties, as well as for younger teens.

These pastoral leaders appear to have captured the cultural experience of youth and young adults who are in transition and expanding their horizons as individuals and peers beyond a local parish. This effort also demonstrates some significant economies of scale in bringing together multiple parishes working on a youth and/or young adult ministry in a regional area. In some instances, collaborating parishes provide a separate monthly eucharistic celebration for young adults through these cross-parochial ministries, recognizing that capturing their interest and commitment to faith may be somewhat different, at this particular point in their lives, than capturing their interest and commitment to a local parish.

Still other pastoral leaders use digital ministries and Web-based media to reach youth and young adults. These vary from age-appropriate and appealing Web sites to podcasts of weekly homilies designed to reach young adults in the media through which they already communicate on a daily basis. This willingness to go beyond parish borders and parish resources to respond to the difficult cultural challenge of engaging youth and young adults is a "first principle" or "best practice" evident among the thought leaders who participated in the symposia.

Regional Collaboration among Parishes

In addition to a cross-parochial commitment to a ministry for youth and young adults, pastoral leaders identified many other specific ways in which they collaborate intentionally with churches to share resources, programs, and pastoral staff whenever possible. These pastoral leaders transcend the boundaries of each parish and recognize that the church of the future may provide a more regional or collaborative identity that includes, and goes beyond, a local parish presence.

These pastoral leaders often share cross-parochial adult formation programs, as well as justice ministry, on a regional, metropolitan, or citywide basis in order to achieve their mission and conserve resources. In some cases, this identity as a regional church became the driving force for reorganizing a cluster of local parishes to provide a more comprehensive regional ministry. These parishes and their leaders demonstrate an awareness of the local church as a community of communities.

One such regional ministry in New England comprises a cluster of parishes that have restructured themselves to provide a single ministry staff, including multiple priests, as a team serving multiple parish communities. This integrated pastoral team is a striking example of intentional regional collaboration that provides campus ministry, comprehensive youth ministry, adult formation and catechesis across parishes, and parish worship sites at local churches. The notion of regional collaboration among parishes is an essential element of their pastoral practice. These "thought leaders" see regional collaboration among parish communities not only in practical terms but also in the context of a collegial church seeking to engage and transform the society as "salt and light."

Structural Commitment to Justice

A commitment to a formal justice ministry was evident in the practice of thought leaders as they described the engagement of their local parishes with their local geographic communities and the world. This is demonstrated either by a high level parish organization such as a parish commission, or in the tithing of parish resources, including time and talent, to the service of those beyond the parish.

These pastoral leaders are highly cognizant of the role and responsibility of the church in the public square. Consequently, they tend to define their commitments to justice as a constitutive outreach to the unique circumstances of their local and even global communities. In some cases, this involves an outreach to the poor or disenfranchised. In other cases, this means partnerships to work on socially difficult issues such as the right-to-life debate. Some of these parishes have developed partnerships with civic groups and churches of other denominations to address the social conditions of their local communities. Some churches draw financial resources from the top line of parish income to contribute to or even "tithe" to ministries beyond the parish.

What is distinctive in their practices is their structural and formal commitment to justice as a presence of the local church in the world. This structural commitment often engages parishioners in sharing their expertise and their sense of community through mission trips to a second- or third-world country to provide food, housing, or healthcare.

The forms of this structural commitment to justice are varied and highly dependent upon the local circumstances of these pastoral leaders and their parish communities. However, this structural commitment to justice is apparent as a "first principle" or best practice reflecting the vitality of their parishes and their commitment to live the word incarnated in their local settings.

Accountability and Transparency in Parish Administration

Some parish pastors who participated in the regional symposia were identified as significant "thought leaders" in determining greater standards for accountability and transparency in parish administration. Often such pastors oversee large communities, budgets, and staff. Their commitment to a higher standard of conduct and leadership is apparent in their administrative vision, as well as in their pastoral practice.

Many pastors have established the practice of publishing parish budgets for review by the community at the beginning and end of each fiscal year. Others have established ethical standards of conduct in dealing with their pastoral staff. Many have adopted formal personnel practices, including job descriptions, regular performance reviews, compensation studies, professional development planning, and training appropriate to the role. Among these leaders there is a strong commitment to just processes and practices as a ministry of the church.

These pastoral leaders appear to have embraced the reality of earning and maintaining the trust of their parishioners and their collaborators through strong systems of accountability, which define excellence in any organization. While accountability and transparency in parish administration have been difficult for many dioceses and parishes, these pastoral leaders have demonstrated a well-integrated sense of the stewardship of parish resources, the spiritual vitality of parish life, and the ethical standards of professional conduct for those in their employment. This commitment to accountability and transparency was an evident best practice among thought leaders in the symposia.

This chapter has outlined twelve best practices for parish excellence that provide an interesting glimpse into a practical, behavioral, and pastoral notion of what constitutes a healthy and vital parish. This notion of best practice may not necessarily reflect the most common practices among pastoral leaders. In fact, one may be challenged to find any individual parish community that fully demonstrates excellence in each of these twelve areas. Taken as a whole, however, they represent the ways in which these thought leaders are beginning to build a future for their communities that is sustainable, vibrant, and faithful to the rich theological and pastoral heritage for which they are faithful stewards. They seem motivated to live out the imperative "By their fruits you will know them."

9

Recommendations for Pastoral Planning

The Emerging Models of Pastoral Leadership Project represented a two-year effort, convening pastoral leaders from eight regions throughout the United States. These pastoral leaders represented diverse parish circumstances, diverse leadership roles, and various levels of experience within the parish. Consequently, the implications of their perspectives for pastoral planning are beneficial to parish leaders in other settings. Their practices may serve as examples to others who wish to strengthen the current vitality and stability of their own communities.

In the broad field of strategic planning, it is well documented that organizations that have a formal long-term plan for the future and use that plan to guide their day-to-day efforts across multiple years have a higher success rate than organizations that do not function with a plan. Sometimes, this day-to-day functioning without a plan is referred to as "leadership by trial and error" or "leadership by the tyranny of the urgent." In other words, what drives current practices in parish life is an exclusive reliance on current circumstances or what was done in the past. A more proactive approach would be to establish a long-term plan for the future, at times working with others to promote a sense of vitality and stability.

This chapter will look at the following four recommendations for pastoral planning, which are consistent with the findings of the regional symposia and the experiences of participating leaders:

- Conduct a parish self-assessment against established benchmarks or best practices.
- Develop a five-year parish strategy for the future that integrates various ministries into a coherent plan.
- Align parish staff and lay volunteers with defined ministry strategies.
- Align resources based upon ministry strategies.

Conduct a Parish Assessment against Benchmarks or Best Practices

There are many ways that organizations—including parishes—can conduct a self-assessment as part of a long-range strategic or pastoral plan. These often include surveys of the entire parish, focus groups among different interest groups within the parish, and the use of a strategic planning study team within the parish. All these methods are useful and helpful. However, self-assessment efforts can be strengthened by utilizing an established set of benchmarks or best practices against which to measure questions and criteria.

It is possible to use the best practices for pastoral excellence that appear in Chapter 8 of this book as a means of conducting a parish self-assessment. Once again, the method of assessment could involve a variety of approaches, including the use of parish surveys, focus groups of interested parishioners, or a parish study team.

Following is an outline of benchmarking questions a parish could use, based upon the findings of the regional symposia for pastoral excellence. These benchmarking questions are organized within the twelve best practice areas identified in the previous chapter.

Sacramentality of parish life as a eucharistic community

- What is the quality of our eucharistic liturgies, including Sundays, holy days, and special occasions? Do our music and homilies offer a prayerful spirit of hospitality and welcome?
- What additional investments does the parish need to make to strengthen the quality of its eucharistic liturgies?
- What other forms of prayer and worship do we undertake as a parish and how might they be strengthened to enhance our overall sense of sacramentality and the worship life of the parish?
- How do we measure parishioner satisfaction with the quality of our eucharistic liturgies and other forms of worship and prayer?
- What are the strengths and weaknesses of each of our areas of sacramental catechesis, including the RCIA and our various sacramental programs?

Total ministering community

- How do we engage members of the parish in service to one another as a parish community?

- How do we engage the parish members in service beyond the parish in a spirit of discipleship to the world and other communities?
- What are ways to strengthen our involvement of parishioners in the life of the parish?
- How diverse and representative are the leadership groups of parishioners actively involved in parish life and ministry?

Formation of lay ministers

- What is the quality of our current formation of lay leaders within the parish community?
- How are we currently providing for the formation of lay leaders for the parish of the future?
- How well do we access diocesan programs and resources to assist in the lay formation of our parish leaders?
- How well do we access the resources of the wider Catholic community—including local Catholic colleges and universities—to assist in the formation of lay leaders?
- As a parish, how effectively do we promote formal programs for vocation awareness?

Pastor or parish life coordinator as facilitator and agent of change

- Who are the leaders within our parish who act formally as facilitators and agents of change for our planning and consensus-building activities?

- How do we provide adequate training and support to those individuals who play this role of facilitator and change agent?
- If not the pastor or parish life coordinator, how do we ensure that we have the needed resources within the parish for planning, problem solving, and conflict resolution?
- What are some concrete ways we can improve our preparedness for change within our parish community?

Pastoral staff as leadership teams that enable ministry

- What are the concrete ways in which our pastoral staff functions as a team?
- What are the frequency and forms of our prayer and formation together as a pastoral team?
- How do we provide time for training each year in the skills that will make us a more effective pastoral team?
- What are our levels of expertise and skills in enabling and assisting the gifts of others to emerge?
- How do we help members of our pastoral team work more effectively in enabling the gifts of others if this is not their innate skill or experience?

The emergent multiculturalism as grace

- What are tangible and concrete images and symbols within our parish community and facilities that reflect diverse cultures, ethnicity, and economic diversity?
- How do we ritualize and celebrate diversity in our worship?

- How do we ritualize and celebrate diversity in social gatherings?
- In what ways can we work with other parishes and communities to strengthen our awareness and appreciation of diversity?
- As a parish, what are some ways we could become more welcoming to others culturally, racially, and socioeconomically?

Lifelong catechesis

- For each of our catechetical ministry areas and programs, what level of outreach and impact do we have in the parish among those eligible to participate in these programs?
- What are the strengths of our catechetical ministry areas or programs, and how can they be improved in the future?
- What are ways to more effectively integrate our catechetical programs to present a seamless and lifelong picture of catechesis as part of the experience of a faith community?
- How do we integrate our catechetical efforts for lifelong formation with the sacramental and worship life of the parish?
- How do we currently use technology and how will we need to use technology in the future to more effectively educate our parishioners in their faith lives?
- What additional resources at the diocesan, local university and college level, or among other parishes

could we access to strengthen our lifelong commitment to catechesis?

Intentional and proactive outreach to individuals and households

- Beyond direct mail and weekly Mass, what forms of regular contact do we have with each parishioner and parish household?
- What is the frequency of our direct outreach and contact with individuals and households in the parish?
- What are the forums we use regularly to acquaint our members with the overall vision, values, and direction of the parish, as well as the programs and services it offers?
- How can we utilize technology more effectively in our parish to identify the needs of our members and to rally their support?
- What structures do we have in place to oversee and facilitate our proactive outreach to individuals and households?

Regional ministry to youth and young adults

- What is our level of outreach to youth in the parish as a percentage of the number of youth who are currently in our parish households?
- What is our level of outreach to young adults in the parish who are in their twenties and thirties as a percentage of the membership of these age groups?
- What are ways we can collaborate with other churches to reach out more effectively to youth and young adults?

- What are the concrete ways that we create a visible presence in the liturgical life of the parish for youth and young adult leaders?
- How can we harness technology more effectively as a means to reach youth and young adults with the communication tools they are most likely to use?

Regional collaboration among parishes

- What ministries of the parish could be shared with other parishes in a five- to ten-year horizon?
- What efforts within the deanery, vicariate, or diocese could we access to visibly promote shared ministries?
- How do we inform members of the parish of the real need for future collaboration among ministries and shared resources?
- How can we more effectively play a leadership role among our neighboring church communities in promoting regional collaboration as a community of communities?

Structural commitment to justice

- How do we focus and express our commitment to justice as a parish?
- What are the concrete programs for justice and outreach beyond the parish that we currently sponsor?
- What percentage of parish resources—including income and time of parish staff—are devoted to justice ministries?

- How are we utilizing the social justice teachings of the church to educate parishioners on justice as a constitutive element of the parish?
- What are some concrete ways we could provide more effective leadership as a parish in chosen justice ministries?

Accountability and transparency in parish administration

- What financial policies do we have in place and how consistent are they with effective business practices and diocesan policies?
- What parish personnel policies do we have in place and how consistent are they with effective business practices and diocesan policies?
- How do we provide annual planning for the compensation of parish employees?
- How do we provide adequate training for parish staff who are employees?
- How do we comply with all legal mandates for the protection of minor children participating in our programs?

Develop a Five-Year Plan for Parish Ministries

The process of pastoral planning involves setting priorities and directions for the future. There are numerous planning models available through planning consultants, Internet resources, business schools, and dioceses that have established parish planning methods and templates. The following elements are common among effective parish planning models and should provide an outline for an effective pastoral plan for the parish community. It is most effective if participation in developing the five-year strategy as part of the pastoral plan is broadened to include parish leaders who represent diverse groups within the parish.

Develop a parish vision

A parish vision represents the destination for any parish community along the journey. In a parish context, this vision may be difficult to articulate. A vision should express the optimum condition a parish attempts to create for its members. It is the place we would like each member to be. The following vision statement is an interesting example of a local parish that worked hard to create a concise, clear, and consistent vision for their parish community:

Vision

We strive to be Spirit-filled with God as the center of our lives, boldly proclaiming Christ and the Catholic tradition through our actions and word.[20]

Develop a parish mission

For those striving toward a parish vision, the parish mission statement expresses the unique characteristics and contributions of a local community. This articulation of contributions as well as capabilities is often expressed in a statement of beliefs about the parish that elicits the best feelings and convictions of its members. One test of an effective mission is its ability to recruit like-minded parishioners, eliciting from them an emotional response that says, "This is my mission, too!" While there are numerous mission statements, the following mission of a Catholic community reflects an interesting process of discernment to articulate the distinctive and unique commitments of a parish:

Mission

We, the Catholic community of Church of the Ascension, are drawn together by our love of Christ as the center of our individual lives, families, community, and ministry. We commit ourselves to being a praying, teaching, caring, serving sign of God's presence to each other and to the world around us. We cooperate in building the kingdom of God by

- *living our Catholic faith and nurturing its growth;*
- *extending a spirit of welcome and belonging in our prayer, liturgy, sacrament, and mission;*
- *accepting and cherishing the dignity of each person;*
- *working in partnership with individuals, churches, and community in service to others.*[21]

Develop a set of ministry core strategies

All models of strategic pastoral planning suggest refining and focusing the major priorities of the future into a handful of five to seven major strategic priorities or directions. For purposes of this chapter, we will refer to these as "ministry core strategies." These ministry core strategies often reflect a "one-page plan" for the parish under which all ministries of the parish can find a home by supporting one of the main ministry strategies. It is often a challenge to consolidate and refine the focus of a parish to five to seven critical areas.

Develop a set of ministry objectives and initiatives for each ministry core strategy

An effective pastoral plan includes concrete priorities, initiatives, or outcomes to be achieved within a five-year period. Under each of the ministry core strategies, objectives and initiatives are recommended for implementation during the time frame of the plan (e.g., five years). These objectives and initiatives should represent concrete commitments to action for the future. These commitments to action could reflect a continuation of existing parish efforts, a redirection of existing parish efforts, or new parish initiatives. It is often difficult to eliminate current priorities in favor of more important priorities for the future. However, this is part of the challenge of an effective pastoral plan.

Develop a set of performance indicators

Within community service, not-for-profit, and church settings, it is often difficult to establish specific performance indicators. It may be important to remember that faith is a performative virtue, meaning the measure of faith is not in words, but in actions and deeds. Consequently, performance indicators are equally a part of a pastoral plan as they would be in a strategic plan for any particular business.

A limited number of performance indicators may be preferable to a long laundry list, but an effective pastoral plan should include measurable, concrete, and meaningful indicators, such as the percentage of growth in members of the parish, the percentage of growth in contributions to the parish, the percentage of growth in service beyond the parish, and the increased percentage of parishioners involved in the worship life of the parish. While some may believe these types of indicators do not adequately reflect a faith community, it should be remembered that parishes are also human organizations and "what gets measured gets accomplished." There is an African tribal expression: "As you pray, keep walking!"

Develop an annual action plan for each ministry core strategy area engaging parish leaders

No pastoral plan would be complete without specific commitments to action. These commitments to action are often best articulated annually with a clear description of key decisions and actions, their timetables for implementation, and those individuals or groups responsible for implementing these actions. It is often helpful to align action plans with each ministry core strategy so that each ministry core strategy has its own set of actions with timetables and responsibilities for completion. The most effective action plans engage members of commissions and committees within the parish to assist the staff in developing the recommended actions for the future. Larger communities may have action plans that are developed and monitored by a key staff person and lay commission.

Align Parish Staff and Lay Leaders with Defined Ministry Core Strategies

One of the significant challenges of any pastoral plan is to align the people leadership resources with the priorities articulated in the plan. It is not uncommon for a pastoral plan to be well crafted, yet placed on the shelf as a "vinyl binder plan." The challenge to any pastoral plan is that it becomes a "living binder plan." This often involves the difficult task of reviewing staff and lay volunteer responsibilities to determine how they can be more effectively redirected to support pastoral planning priorities. This can be a painful process of letting go of prior efforts or projects that appeal to individuals but may not contribute effectively to the growth of the entire parish. All programs and projects have a life cycle, with ups and downs and eventual calls for a redirection of leadership to anticipate the next horizon. Consequently, it takes considerable skills to align parish staff and volunteer resources with the ministry core strategies of the future.

Within each five-year planning horizon, a table of organization of the staffing structure could be developed to realign staffing resources to support the ministry core strategies articulated in the pastoral plan. In keeping with symposia findings, staff roles may continually evolve to call forth the gifts of others to provide service to the parish and beyond. The same exercise can also be done for all parish lay-led organizations and groups. An interesting exercise for any parish would be to develop a one-page structure for all parish organizations and groups that aligns them with the ministry core strategies of the parish.

In some very successful planning experiences, parishes have established top-level ministry commissions or advisory boards that support the parish council. Each of these commissions or advisory boards is aligned with one of the major ministry areas of the parish. This is a very familiar experience of parishes in the areas of education commissions, liturgical commissions, and social justice commissions. The leadership pattern of establishing a formal lay commission for each ministry area can often yield great benefits, not only to implementing the pastoral plan, but also to developing a ministering community and common commitment to leadership among increasingly greater numbers of parish members.

Align Financial Resources Based on Ministry Core Strategies

Aligning the financial resources of the parish with the ministry core strategies and priorities for the future presents a formidable challenge. This is not unlike the challenge of aligning staff and volunteer resources with the new priorities and needs that are emerging from a pastoral plan.

During a pastoral planning cycle, it can often be helpful to develop a five-year budget forecast that presents a gradual shift of resources to more effectively align parish financial commitments with established ministry core strategies. Certainly within parish life, foxholes are easily established to protect current investments and current priorities. This is often a hurdle, particularly when aligning those resources that are expended outside the parish to focus on social justice ministries. It is easy to appease multiple "pet needs" by spreading few resources over many areas.

One particular parish community represented at the symposia had actually taken the step of investing accountability and responsibility with its leadership commissions for the annual assignment of resources within their ministry areas. This represents a very substantive commitment of this parish community, not only to lay leadership, but also to a continual commitment to reexamine the financial resources of the parish as they are allocated to support important ministries.

However parishes achieve this realignment of resources, it is important to remember that the financial contributions of parishioners are intended to support the life and work of the parish. To the extent that the alignment of these financial resources is not directed in the best interest of the parish as a whole, the community will undoubtedly be limited in its ability to achieve its major ministry strategies and priorities for the future.

Throughout this chapter, some very concrete examples have been suggested regarding the implications of pastoral planning that have resulted from the leadership experiences of participants in the regional symposia. Wherever a parish finds itself, the most important thing is to get started on the process. However simple, however basic, every parish community of whatever size can begin the process of envisioning and planning for a preferred future. Sometimes this future will require greater reliance on others, and at other times it will require facing very difficult challenges, such as redirecting programs, creating new ministries, or closing existing ministries or parish facilities. In all these efforts, it is important to remember the following prayer of St. Paul to the Ephesians, which may suggest why we strive to continually review and refresh our communities and understanding of church:

That is why I kneel before the Father from whom every family in heaven and on earth takes its name and I pray that he will bestow on you gifts in keeping with the riches of His glory. May He strengthen you inwardly through the working of His Spirit, may Christ dwell in your heart through faith, and may charity be the root and foundation of your life. Thus, you will be able to grasp with all the holy ones the breadth and length and height and depth of Christ's love and experience this love which surpasses all knowledge, so that you may attain to the fullness of God himself. (Eph. 3:14–19)

Appendix:
Symposia Participant Profile

Respondent Profile*

Regional Symposia	Participants by Region	% of Total Participants	Respondents by Region	% of Total Respondents
Pacific Northwest	60	11%	49	11%
Upper Midwest	85	16%	53	12%
Northeast	69	13%	50	12%
Mid-Atlantic	52	9%	52	12%
Southeast	94	18%	80	18%
Southwest	57	11%	50	12%
South	57	11%	53	12%
North Central	55	10%	46	11%
Total	**529**		**433**	

82% of symposia participants completed discussion guides.

Symposia Respondent Groups

Respondent Groups	Respondents by Group	% of Total Respondents
Pastors	82	19%
Parish Life Coordinators	44	10%
Deacons	37	9%
Pastoral Associates	71	16%
Parish Pastoral Council Reps	30	7%
Diocesan Reps	88	20%
Other	60	14%
(Left Blank)	21	5%
Total Respondents	**433**	

Respondents by Gender

Gender	Respondents by Group	% of Total Respondents
Male	218	50%
Female	193	45%
(Left Blank)	22	5%
Total Respondents	**433**	

Respondents by Age Group

Age Groups	Respondents by Group	% of Total Respondents
Under 29	8	2%
Age 30–39	29	7%
Age 40–49	65	15%
Age 50–59	165	38%
Age 60–69	124	29%
Age 70 and Over	20	5%
(Left Blank)	22	5%
Total Respondents	**433**	

Respondents by Number of Parish Households

Parish Households	Respondents by Group	% of Total Respondents
Under 500	83	19%
501–1200	116	27%
1201–2000	93	21%
Over 2001	103	24%
(Left Blank)	38	9%
Total Respondents	**433**	

Respondents by Highest Level of Education

Highest Level of Education	Respondents by Group	% of Total Respondents
High School Diploma	18	4%
Associate Degree	16	4%
Bachelor Degree	52	12%
Master's Degree	276	64%
Doctorate	41	9%
(Left Blank)	30	7%
Total Respondents	**433**	

Respondents by Parish Structure

Parish Structure	Respondents by Group	% of Total Respondents
Parish with pastor responsible for one parish	202	47%
Parish with pastor responsible for two or more parishes	48	11%
Parish with a team of priests serving as a pastoral team for one or more parishes in accord with Canon 517.1	10	2%
Parish under the care of a parish life coordinator appointed by the bishop in accord with Canon 517.2	31	7%
(Left Blank)	142	33%
Total Respondents	**433**	

Endnotes

1. The Emerging Models of Pastoral Leadership Project, funded by a significant grant from the Lilly Endowment, Inc., was designed to study pastoral leadership in today's parishes and then generate conversation about achieving pastoral excellence. For more about the project visit www.emergingmodels.org.

2. John Paul II, Apostolic Letter, *Novo Millennio Ineunte* (2001), no. 29.

3. NCEA annual statistical report on Catholic Schools, 2007–2008.

4. John Gardner quoted in David Ramey, *Empowering Leadership* (Kansas City: Sheed and Ward, 1991), 76.

5. For example, see Mark Mogilka and Kate Wiskus, *Pastoring Multiple Parishes* (Chicago: Loyola Press, 2009).

6. John Zizioulas quoted by Patricia Fox in *God As Communion* (Collegeville: Liturgical Press, 2001), 83.

7. Patricia Fox, *God As Communion*, 84.

8. Mogilka and Wiskus, *Pastoring Multiple Parishes*, 22.

9. Pope Benedict XVI, "Meeting with Clergy," *Origins*, 37, no. 11 (August 16, 2007): 190.

10. Richard R. Gaillardetz, "The Ecclesiological Foundations of Ministry within an Ordered Communion," in *Ordering the Baptismal Priesthood*, ed. Susan Wood (Collegeville: Liturgical Press, 2003), 29.

11. Robert J. Kaslyn, S.J., "Book II: The People of God (cc. 204–329)," in *New Commentary on the Code of Canon Law*, ed. John Beal, *et al.* (Mahwah, NJ: Paulist Press, 2000), 254.

12. United States Conference of Catholic Bishops, *Co-Workers in the Vineyard of the Lord: A Resource for Guiding the Development of Lay Ecclesial Ministry* (2005), 8.

13. David DeLambo, "In Search of Pastoral Excellence," *Church*, NY, Summer, 2007, p. 3.

14. *Co-Workers*, 11.

15. William T. Ditewig, "Implementation Strategies for the *New National Directory of Deacons*," in *Today's Deacon: Contemporary Issues and Cross Currents* (Mahwah, NJ: Paulist Press, 2006), 44.

16. Ibid., 45.

17. Katarina Schuth, *Priestly Ministry in Multiple Parishes* (Collegeville, MN: Liturgical Press, 2006), 3.

18. Kathy Hendricks and Brian Reynolds, "Canon 517.2: An Established and Emerging Model," accessed at http://www.emerging models.org/doc/PLCs%20Summit%20Report.pdf, April 7, 2009.

19. James A. Coriden, "Parish Pastoral Leaders: Canonical Structures and Practical Questions," accessed at http://www.emergingmodels .org, April 7, 2009.

20. Used with the permission of Church of the Ascension, Kettering, Ohio, Strategic Plan, April 2008.

21. Used with the permission of Church of the Ascension, Kettering, Ohio, Strategic Plan, April 2008.

About the Project

From 2003 through 2008, the Emerging Models of Pastoral Leadership Project, a collaborative effort of six national organizations, funded by the Lilly Endowment, Inc., conducted national research on the emerging models of parish and parish leadership. Their objective was to find the best practices and ideas of pastoral leaders in order to share them with pastoral leaders throughout the country. During this period the Project conducted eight regional leadership symposia. Dioceses were asked to send their most creative thought leaders to these gatherings to share their experience. This book provides an analysis and summary of their ideas and practices.

More information on these studies is available on the Emerging Models Project website: http://www.emerging models.org.

The six partner organizations of the Emerging Models of Pastoral Leadership Project, funded by the Lilly Endowment, Inc., are the following:

- National Association for Lay Ministry (NALM)
- Conference for Pastoral Planning and Council Development (CPPCD)
- National Association of Church Personnel Administrators (NACPA)
- National Association of Diaconate Directors (NADD)
- National Catholic Young Adult Ministry Association (NCYAMA)
- National Federation of Priests' Councils (NFPC)

About the Authors

Marti Jewell D.Min., served as the director of the Emerging Models of Pastoral Leadership Project from 2003 through the completion of the first phase of the Project in 2009. Now an assistant professor of theology in the School of Ministry at the University of Dallas, she offers keynotes and workshops on the findings of the Project, addressing key ministry issues across the country.

David Ramey has been president of Strategic Leadership Associates, Inc., since 1987. He formerly served as president of Bergamo Center for Lifelong Learning, a national conference and training center in Dayton, Ohio. Dave has completed the book *Empowering Leaders*, published by Sheed and Ward and now in its second printing. His Strategic Leadership Assessment & Profile is now available.

Dave has served as a strategic planning and organizational development consultant to business, government, human services, foundations, national organizations, conference centers, and universities throughout the United States. In 2001 he received NASA's Public Service Medal, the agency's highest civilian award. His NASA clients have included the Marshall Space Flight Center, Langley Research Center, and the National Space Science and Technology Center.

Dave received a BA from Marquette University and a master's degree in education from Loyola University of Chicago. He also holds a Certificate in Training and Consulting from the University of Wisconsin in Madison. Dave frequently offers regional and national workshops on leadership development and strategic planning.

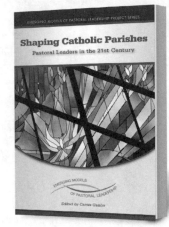

Parish Life Coordinators

Profile of an Emerging Ministry

Kathy Hendricks

Paperback • 120 pages
ISBN: 978-0-8294-2640-9
$11.95

With the growing shortage of priests in the United States, a significant number of parishes are being entrusted to religious, deacons, and lay pastoral leaders. Sometimes called parish life coordinators (PLCs), these men and women are bringing new life and purpose to parishes. *Parish Life Coordinators* explains how the PLC model works, shares best practices from parishes using the model, and offers practical implementation ideas that will help parishes without a priest successfully serve the ever-increasing pastoral needs of their people.

LOYOLA PRESS.
A JESUIT MINISTRY

Phone: 800-621-1008 • Fax: 773-281-0555 • Visit: www.loyolapress.com/store

Pastoring Multiple Parishes

Mark Mogilka
and Kate Wiskus

Paperback • 192 pages
ISBN: 978-0-8294-2649-6
$11.95

Nearly half of U.S. parishes and missions currently share their pastor with another parish or mission. In *Pastoring Multiple Parishes*, Mark Mogilka and Kate Wiskus share with readers what works and what doesn't when parishes must share a pastor, offering practical advice to help Catholics see this growing trend as a wonderful opportunity for future stability and growth of the faith.

LOYOLA PRESS.
A JESUIT MINISTRY

EMERGING MODELS
OF PASTORAL LEADERSHIP
A Joint Project Funded by the Lilly Endowment, Inc.

Phone: 800-621-1008 • Fax: 773-281-0555 • Visit: www.loyolapress.com/store

The Next Generation of Pastoral Leaders

What the Church Needs to Know

Dean R. Hoge and
Marti R. Jowoll

Paperback • 160 pages • ISBN: 978-0-8294-2650-2 • $11.95

Based on a survey conducted by the renowned late sociologist Dr. Dean R. Hoge, *The Next Generation of Pastoral Leaders* provides a unique glimpse into the thinking and attitudes of young Catholic adults as it relates to pastoral ministry. The findings contained in this book are essential for anyone in Catholic ministry to understand if the Church is to successfully develop both lay and ordained pastoral leaders for the future, and, more immediately, if the Church is to involve young people in parish life and campus ministry today.

LOYOLAPRESS.
A JESUIT MINISTRY

Phone: 800-621-1008 • Fax: 773-281-0555 • Visit: www.loyolapress.com/store